Phonics and Word Recognition Quick Checks

Table of Contents

Table of Contents

Table of Contents

Introduction

Program Overview

The *Benchmark Advance* program has ten units per grade in Grades K–6. There are ten knowledge strands on which the program revolves. Each three-week unit focuses on a Unit Topic and an Essential Question, which both relate back to the overall knowledge strand. Throughout the school year, students engage with texts in whole- and small-group settings, developing their phonics skills and applying the new strategies in context.

These Phonics and Word Recognition assessments are designed to help you evaluate your students' awareness of phonics concepts and to provide a tool for determining when it is appropriate to use intervention materials. Below is a summary of the key *Benchmark Advance* resources used in the intervention cycle.

Teacher's Resource System and Student Reading Materials

The Teacher's Resource System and associated student reading serve as the core of the *Benchmark Advance* program. This material supports day-to-day instruction throughout the school year.

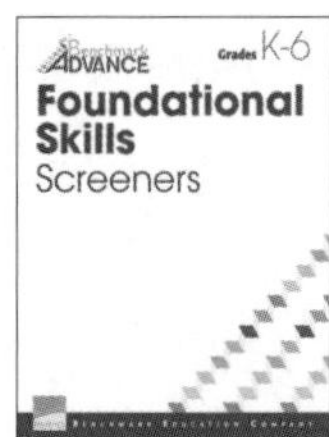

Foundational Skills Screeners

Foundational Skills Screeners consists of quick tests focused on foundational reading skills, including recognizing root words, identifying affixes, and recognizing sound patterns. *Foundational Skills Screeners* provides an efficient way to assess the general understanding of the class. Based on students' scores, you can shape instruction to meet developing areas of need before students fall behind.

Quick Checks to Intervention

The five Quick Checks consist of short, skill-based assessments designed to help you evaluate student command in key skill and knowledge areas. You may use students' performance on the Quick Checks to inform your decision of when to implement intervention. The Resource Map in the beginning of every Quick Checks book leads you to the intervention lesson(s) that focus on the skill(s) assessed in each Quick Check test.

***Benchmark Advance* Intervention:**
Phonics and Word Recognition

The grade-specific, skill-based lessons in each Intervention book provide you with instruction and practice needed to raise struggling students to on-level proficiency. Designed to integrate with Quick Checks, these intervention resources enable you to pinpoint trouble areas and support students as they build the skill set they need for complete understanding.

Description of the Assessments

Phonics and word recognition involve sound-print correspondence: making the connection between the sounds we hear and the letters on the page. The assessments in this book evaluate students on a number of phonics skills, including letter recognition, identifying consonant blends and digraphs, and syllabication.

There are two assessment pages per skill—except in the High-Frequency Words section, which is organized by unit. The skill that the Quick Check assesses can be found in the table of contents and in the Resource Map, which begins on page xxvi. The assessments are intended for individual, one-on-one administration. You may make a copy of the test for each student you plan to assess.

Skills in this book are generally presented in sequence, mimicking the order in the day-to-day instruction of the Teacher's Resource System. However, students may be assessed on a given skill at any time, based on what is happening in the classroom or the particular needs of the student.

Every assessment may be used more than once, if needed. In most cases, the second assessment page tests different aspects of the skill or uses a different approach. In some assessments, you may note one or two items that do not test the skill listed at the top of the page. For example, in an assessment on Initial Consonant *m*, you may see an item testing Initial Consonant *t*. This ensures that the student being assessed is responding based on knowledge, not memory or repetition.

Teacher Administration and Answers

The Teacher Administration and Answers section that follows this Introduction serves as a teacher script and an answer key. After you hand the Quick Check to the student, refer to the prompt in the Directions column. The prompts reflect the difficulty level of the skill being tested. The higher the skill level, the more that is required of the student.

When the student completes the assessment, collect the test and mark correct and incorrect responses on the student's paper. Place a check mark next to correct answers and an X beside incorrect answers. Add the total number of correct answers to determine the student's score. Each Quick Check has a score box for recording the student's results.

Quick Check to Phonics and Word Recognition Intervention

The score on each Quick Check may be used for record keeping or grading, but the final score on each page is less important than how the student responds along the way. Ultimately, these Quick Checks are intended as formative assessments to help you monitor students' progress and adapt instruction to each individual's needs.

Considering responses from the class as a whole helps determine when to move on to new or more difficult tasks. Carefully observe each student's phonics proficiency and the student's use of word recognition skills, documenting both lessons taught and skills mastered.

Using Quick Checks to Help Guide Intervention Decisions

Based on your student's score, you may decide to offer the student resources in the *Benchmark Advance* intervention kit. The Resource Map that follows this Introduction aligns the skills being assessed to the Phonics and Word Recognition Intervention lessons.

If the student scores . . .	**Then . . .**
between 80% and 100%	Move on to the next Quick Check or skill.
between 66% and 80%	Consider administering the Quick Check again. Continue monitoring the student during future Quick Checks.
below 66%	Use intervention resources shown in the Resource Map to provide the student with opportunities to remediate skills.

Grades K–2

Teacher Administration and Answers

Quick Check	Directions	Answers
1	**Say:** *Point to row 1. Say the letters in the row.* Repeat for rows 2–5. Use the Answers column to follow along as the student reads. Mark correct and incorrect answers on the student's paper per row.	1. b t c q w y 2. a s f r j g 3. l m d i z 4. v u h n x 5. k e o p
2	**Say:** *Point to row 1. Say the letters in the row.* Repeat for rows 2–5. Use the Answers column to follow along as the student reads. Mark correct and incorrect answers on the student's paper per row.	1. L E G P T K 2. D U W H C X 3. M Q A N O 4. Y F Z S J 5. V R I B
3	**Say:** *Point to the picture in row 1. It is a picture of a moon. Circle the letter that you hear at the beginning of moon.* Repeat for rows 2–5. [2. mitten; 3. mouse; 4. tape; 5. man]	1. m 4. t 2. m 5. m 3. m
4	• **Say:** *Point to the picture in row 1. It is a picture of a monkey. Circle the word that has the same <u>beginning</u> sound as monkey.* Repeat for rows 2–3. [2. map; 3. mouse] • **Say:** *Point to the picture in row 4. It is a picture of a broom. Circle the word that has the same <u>ending</u> sound as broom.* Repeat for row 5. [5. jam]	1. mop 4. dam 2. mat 5. hum 3. mad
5	**Say:** *Point to the picture in row 1. It is a picture of a horse and there is an arrow pointing to the tail. Circle the letter that you hear at the beginning of tail.* Repeat for rows 2–5. [2. top; 3. mitt; 4. tub; 5. toe]	1. t 4. t 2. t 5. t 3. m
6	• **Say:** *Point to the picture in row 1. It is a picture of a tack. Circle the word that has the same <u>beginning</u> sound as tack.* Repeat for rows 2–3. [2. two; 3. team] • **Say:** *Point to the picture in row 4. It is a picture of a net. Circle the word that has the same <u>ending</u> sound as net.* Repeat for row 5. [5. pot]	1. tell 4. get 2. tan 5. wet 3. tap
7	**Say:** *Point to the picture in row 1. It is a picture of a nose. Circle the letter that you hear at the beginning of nose.* Repeat for rows 2–5. [2. mop; 3. nail; 4. neck (boy, with an arrow pointing to his neck); 5. nest]	1. n 4. n 2. m 5. n 3. n
8	• **Say:** *Point to the picture in row 1. It is a picture of a net. Circle the word that has the same <u>beginning</u> sound as net.* Repeat for rows 2–3. [2. nut; 3. nine] • **Say:** *Point to the picture in row 4. It is a picture of a pen. Circle the word that has the same <u>ending</u> sound as pen.* Repeat for row 5. [5. fin (shark, with an arrow pointing to the fin)]	1. no 4. tin 2. nip 5. bun 3. not
9	**Say:** *Point to the picture in row 1. It is a picture of a pig. Circle the letter that you hear at the beginning of pig.* Repeat for rows 2–5. [2. pool; 3. mouse; 4. pan; 5. peas]	1. p 4. p 2. p 5. p 3. m

Quick Check	Directions	Answers	
10	• **Say:** *Point to the picture in row 1. It is a picture of a pin. Circle the word that has the same <u>beginning</u> sound as pin.* Repeat for rows 2–3. [2. pond; 3. piano] • **Say:** *Point to the picture in row 4. It is a picture of a hoop. Circle the word that has the same <u>ending</u> sound as hoop.* Repeat for row 5. [5. cup]	1. pad 2. pet 3. pit	4. rip 5. tap
11	**Say:** *Point to the picture in row 1. It is a picture of a bat. Circle the letter that you hear at the beginning of bat.* Repeat for rows 2–5. [2. bug; 3. bowl; 4. pot; 5. bus]	1. b 2. b 3. b	4. p 5. b
12	• **Say:** *Point to the picture in row 1. It is a picture of a bell. Circle the word that has the same <u>beginning</u> sound as bell.* Repeat for rows 2–3. [2. bike; 3. bag] • **Say:** *Point to the picture in row 4. It is a picture of a cub. Circle the word that has the same <u>ending</u> sound as cub.* Repeat for row 5. [5. crab]	1. bud 2. ban 3. bit	4. dab 5. lob
13	**Say:** *Point to the picture in row 1. It is a picture of a dog. Circle the letter that you hear at the beginning of dog.* Repeat for rows 2–5. [2. ball; 3. door; 4. duck; 5. desk]	1. d 2. b 3. d	4. d 5. d
14	• **Say:** *Point to the picture in row 1. It is a picture of a dock. Circle the word that has the same <u>beginning</u> sound as dock.* Repeat for rows 2–3. [2. dig; 3. dime] • **Say:** *Point to the picture in row 4. It is a picture of a seed. Circle the word that has the same <u>ending</u> sound as seed.* Repeat for row 5. [5. bed]	1. dip 2. den 3. dot	4. wed 5. rod
15	**Say:** *Point to the picture in row 1. It is a picture of a goat. Circle the letter that you hear at the beginning of goat.* Repeat for rows 2–5. [2. goose; 3. gate; 4. pan; 5. girl]	1. g 2. g 3. g	4. p 5. g
16	• **Say:** *Point to the picture in row 1. It is a picture of a gift. Circle the word that has the same <u>beginning</u> sound as gift.* Repeat for rows 2–3. [2. game; 3. ghost] • **Say:** *Point to the picture in row 4. It is a picture of a rug. Circle the word that has the same <u>ending</u> sound as rug.* Repeat for row 5. [5. frog]	1. got 2. gap 3. get	4. fig 5. wag
17	**Say:** *Point to the picture in row 1. It is a picture of a sun. Circle the letter that you hear at the beginning of sun.* Repeat for rows 2–5. [2. sail; 3. sock; 4. pear; 5. saw]	1. s 2. s 3. s	4. p 5. s
18	**Say:** *Point to row 1. I am going to say a word. Find and circle the word in the row: sip.* Repeat for rows 2–5. [2. sat; 3. sum; 4. sob; 5. sand]	1. sip 2. sat 3. sum	4. sob 5. sand
19	**Say:** *Point to the picture in row 1. It is a picture of a rake. Circle the letter that you hear at the beginning of rake.* Repeat for rows 2–5. [2. moon; 3. ring; 4. road; 5. rose]	1. r 2. m 3. r	4. r 5. r

Grades K–2

Teacher Administration and Answers

Quick Check	Directions	Answers
20	**Say:** *Point to row 1. I am going to say a word. Find and circle the word in the row: ran.* Repeat for rows 2–5. [2. rut; 3. rob; 4. rim; 5. rock]	1. ran 2. rut 3. rob 4. rim 5. rock
21	**Say:** *Point to the picture in row 1. It is a picture of a foot. Circle the letter that you hear at the beginning of foot.* Repeat for rows 2–5. [2. fan; 3. fish; 4. four; 5. rain]	1. f 2. f 3. f 4. f 5. r
22	**Say:** *Point to row 1. I am going to say a word. Find and circle the word in the row: fit.* Repeat for rows 2–5. [2. fun; 3. fog; 4. fed; 5. fake]	1. fit 2. fun 3. fog 4. fed 5. fake
23	**Say:** *Point to the picture in row 1. It is a picture of a cup. Circle the letter that you hear at the beginning of cup.* Repeat for rows 2–5. [2. can; 3. cake; 4. fox; 5. car]	1. c 2. c 3. c 4. f 5. c
24	**Say:** *Point to row 1. I am going to say a word. Find and circle the word in the row: cap.* Repeat for rows 2–5. [2. cut; 3. cob; 4. cot; 5. came]	1. cap 2. cut 3. cob 4. cot 5. came
25	**Say:** *Point to the picture in row 1. It is a picture of a hat. Circle the letter that you hear at the beginning of hat.* Repeat for rows 2–5. [2. tent; 3. house; 4. hen; 5. hand]	1. h 2. t 3. h 4. h 5. h
26	**Say:** *Point to row 1. I am going to say a word. Find and circle the word in the row: hot.* Repeat for rows 2–5. [2. hip; 3. had; 4. hug; 5. him]	1. hot 2. hip 3. had 4. hug 5. him
27	**Say:** *Point to the picture in row 1. It is a picture of a wig. Circle the letter that you hear at the beginning of wig.* Repeat for rows 2–5. [2. hut; 3. web; 4. watch; 5. well]	1. w 2. h 3. w 4. w 5. w
28	**Say:** *Point to row 1. I am going to say a word. Find and circle the word in the row: win.* Repeat for rows 2–5. [2. week; 3. wag; 4. wide; 5. wet]	1. win 2. week 3. wag 4. wide 5. wet
29	**Say:** *Point to the picture in row 1. It is a picture of a lion. Circle the letter that you hear at the beginning of lion.* Repeat for rows 2–5. [2. leg; 3. lip; 4. raft; 5. lemon]	1. l 2. l 3. l 4. r 5. l
30	**Say:** *Point to row 1. I am going to say a word. Find and circle the word in the row: let.* Repeat for rows 2–5. [2. log; 3. lick; 4. lug; 5. land]	1. let 2. log 3. lick 4. lug 5. land
31	**Say:** *Point to the picture in row 1. It is a picture of a jam. Circle the letter that you hear at the beginning of jam.* Repeat for rows 2–5. [2. juice; 3. lamp; 4. jug; 5. jeep]	1. j 2. j 3. l 4. j 5. j
32	**Say:** *Point to row 1. I am going to say a word. Find and circle the word in the row: jet.* Repeat for rows 2–5. [2. jog; 3. Jim; 4. just; 5. jab]	1. jet 2. jog 3. Jim 4. just 5. jab

Quick Check	Directions	Answers
33	**Say:** *Point to the picture in row 1. It is a picture of a key. Circle the letter that you hear at the beginning of key.* Repeat for rows 2–5. [2. king; 3. pear; 4. kite; 5. kick]	1. k 2. k 3. p 4. k 5. k
34	**Say:** *Point to row 1. I am going to say a word. Find and circle the word in the row: kit.* Repeat for rows 2–5. [2. kiss; 3. kale; 4. keen; 5. kid]	1. kit 2. kiss 3. kale 4. keen 5. kid
35	**Say:** *Point to the picture in row 1. It is a picture of a yard. Circle the letter that you hear at the beginning of yard.* Repeat for rows 2–5. [2. yak; 3. yam; 4. yolk (picture of an egg, with an arrow pointing to the yolk); 5. jar]	1. y 2. y 3. y 4. y 5. j
36	**Say:** *Point to row 1. I am going to say a word. Find and circle the word in the row: yet.* Repeat for rows 2–5. [2. yap; 3. yell; 4. yip; 5. yen]	1. yet 2. yap 3. yell 4. yip 5. yen
37	**Say:** *Point to the picture in row 1. It is a picture of a van. Circle the letter that you hear at the beginning of van.* Repeat for rows 2–5. [2. vest; 3. web; 4. violin; 5. vine]	1. v 2. v 3. w 4. v 5. v
38	**Say:** *Point to row 1. I am going to say a word. Find and circle the word in the row: vet.* Repeat for rows 2–5. [2. vast; 3. vane; 4. vim; 5. vote]	1. vet 2. vast 3. vane 4. vim 5. vote
39	**Say:** *Point to row 1. I am going to say a word. Find and circle the word in the row: queen.* Repeat for rows 2–5. [2. quit; 3. quail; 4. quote; 5. quip]	1. queen 2. quit 3. quail 4. quote 5. quip
40	**Say:** *Point to row 1. I am going to say a word. Find and circle the word in the row: quite.* Repeat for rows 2–5. [2. quill; 3. quack; 4. quake; 5. quest]	1. quite 2. quill 3. quack 4. quake 5. quest
41	**Say:** *Point to the picture in row 1. It is a picture of a zebra. Circle the letter that you hear at the beginning of zebra.* Repeat for rows 2–5. [2. zipper; 3. suit; 4. zoo; 5. zero]	1. z 2. z 3. s 4. z 5. z
42	**Say:** *Point to row 1. I am going to say a word. Find and circle the word in the row: zip.* Repeat for rows 2–5. [2. zone; 3. zap; 4. zoom; 5. Zack]	1. zip 2. zone 3. zap 4. zoom 5. Zack
43	**Say:** *Point to the picture in row 1. It is a picture of a box. Circle the letter that you hear at the end of box.* Repeat for rows 2–5. [2. six; 3. book; 4. fox; 5. mix (picture of someone's hand mixing something)]	1. x 2. x 3. k 4. x 5. x
44	**Say:** *Point to row 1. I am going to say a word. Find and circle the word in the row: fix.* Repeat for rows 2–5. [2. sax; 3. mix; 4. Rex; 5. fax]	1. fix 2. sax 3. mix 4. Rex 5. fax

Grades K–2

Teacher Administration and Answers

Quick Check	Directions	Answers	
45	**Say:** *Point to row 1. I am going to say a word. Find and circle the word in the row: hose.* Repeat for rows 2–5. [2. suds; 3. rise; 4. says; 5. his]	1. hose 2. suds 3. rise	4. says 5. his
46	**Say:** *Point to row 1. I am going to say a word. Find and circle the word in the row: wise.* Repeat for rows 2–5. [2. peas; 3. has; 4. rose; 5. sees]	1. wise 2. peas 3. has	4. rose 5. sees
47	**Say:** *Point to row 1. I am going to say a word. Find and circle the word in the row: lock.* Repeat for rows 2–5. [2. duck; 3. kick; 4. neck; 5. pack]	1. lock 2. duck 3. kick	4. neck 5. pack
48	**Say:** *Point to row 1. I am going to say a word. Find and circle the word in the row: pick.* Repeat for rows 2–5. [2. rock; 3. luck; 4. tack; 5. deck]	1. pick 2. rock 3. luck	4. tack 5. deck
49	**Say:** *Point to the picture in row 1. It is a picture of a bell. Circle the letters that you hear at the end of bell.* Repeat for rows 2–5. [2. mitt; 3. cliff; 4. grass; 5. hill]	1. ll 2. tt 3. ff	4. ss 5. ll
50	**Say:** *Point to row 1. I am going to say a word. Find and circle the word in the row: mutt.* Repeat for rows 2–5. [2. pass; 3. cuff; 4. till; 5. less]	1. mutt 2. pass 3. cuff	4. till 5. less
51	**Say:** *Point to the picture in row 1. It is a picture of a clock. Circle the letters that you hear at the beginning of clock.* Repeat for rows 2–5. [2. plug; 3. glove; 4. slide; 5. block]	1. cl 2. pl 3. gl	4. sl 5. bl
52	**Say:** *Point to row 1. I am going to say a word. Find and circle the word in the row: slip.* Repeat for rows 2–5. [2. plum; 3. glad; 4. club; 5. flag]	1. slip 2. plum 3. glad	4. club 5. flag
53	**Say:** *Point to the picture in row 1. It is a picture of a snake. Circle the letters that you hear at the beginning of snake.* Repeat for rows 2–5. [2. ski (picture of a person skiing); 3. swan; 4. star; 5. spoon]	1. sn 2. sk 3. sw	4. st 5. sp
54	**Say:** *Point to row 1. I am going to say a word. Find and circle the word in the row: spot.* Repeat for rows 2–5. [2. snug; 3. smock; 4. swim; 5. skin]	1. spot 2. snug 3. smock	4. swim 5. skin
55	**Say:** *Point to the picture in row 1. It is a picture of a crab. Circle the letters that you hear at the beginning of crab.* Repeat for rows 2–5. [2. grass; 3. drum; 4. truck; 5. frog]	1. cr 2. gr 3. dr	4. tr 5. fr
56	**Say:** *Point to row 1. I am going to say a word. Find and circle the word in the row: trap.* Repeat for rows 2–5. [2. brick; 3. grim; 4. drop; 5. free]	1. trap 2. brick 3. grim	4. drop 5. free

Quick Check	Directions	Answers
57	**Say:** *Point to the picture in row 1. It is a picture of a stream. Circle the letters that you hear at the beginning of stream.* Repeat for rows 2–5. [2. splash (picture of a car making a splash); 3. square; 4. sprout; 5. straw]	1. str 2. spl 3. squ 4. spr 5. str
58	**Say:** *Point to row 1. I am going to say a word. Find and circle the word in the row: strap.* Repeat for rows 2–5. [2. split; 3. spring; 4. squid; 5. spray]	1. strap 2. split 3. spring 4. squid 5. spray
59	**Say:** *Point to the picture in row 1. It is a picture of a vest. Circle the letters that you hear at the end of vest.* Repeat for rows 2–5. [2. hand; 3. tank; 4. lamp; 5. mask]	1. st 2. nd 3. nk 4. mp 5. sk
60	**Say:** *Point to row 1. I am going to say a word. Find and circle the word in the row: went.* Repeat for rows 2–5. [2. jump; 3. last; 4. desk; 5. bank]	1. went 2. jump 3. last 4. desk 5. bank
61	• **Say:** *Point to the picture in row 1. It is a picture of a ship. Circle the letters that you hear at the <u>beginning</u> of ship.* Repeat for row 2. [2. thumb] • **Say:** *Point to the picture in row 3. It is a picture of a ring. Circle the letters that you hear at the <u>end</u> of ring.* Repeat for rows 4–5. [4. path; 5. fish]	1. sh 2. th 3. ng 4. th 5. sh
62	**Say:** *Point to row 1. I am going to say a word. Find and circle the word in the row: wing.* Repeat for rows 2–5. [2. bash; 3. cloth; 4. long; 5. rush]	1. wing 2. bash 3. cloth 4. long 5. rush
63	• **Say:** *Point to the picture in row 1. It is a picture of a whale. Circle the letters that you hear at the <u>beginning</u> of whale.* Repeat for rows 2–3. [2. chin (picture of a boy's face, with an arrow pointing to his chin); 3. chain] • **Say:** *Point to the picture in row 4. It is a picture of a watch. Circle the letters that you hear at the <u>end</u> of watch.* Repeat for row 5. [5. beach]	1. wh 2. ch 3. ch 4. tch 5. ch
64	**Say:** *Point to row 1. I am going to say a word. Find and circle the word in the row: much.* Repeat for rows 2–5. [2. pitch; 3. white; 4. chill; 5. wheel]	1. much 2. pitch 3. white 4. chill 5. wheel
65	• **Say:** *Point to row 1. Circle the word that has the same <u>beginning</u> sound as sip.* Repeat for row 2. [2. jet] • **Say:** *Point to row 3. Circle the word that has the same <u>ending</u> sound as page.* Repeat for rows 4–5. [4. miss; 5. ledge]	1. cent 2. gem 3. ridge 4. race 5. wage
66	**Say:** *Point to row 1. I am going to say a word. Find and circle the word in the row: lace.* Repeat for rows 2–5. [2. judge; 3. rice; 4. stage; 5. badge]	1. lace 2. judge 3. rice 4. stage 5. badge

Grades K–2
Teacher Administration and Answers

Quick Check	Directions	Answers
67	• **Say:** *Point to row 1. Circle the word that has the same* *beginning* *sound as rap.* Repeat for rows 2–3. [2. nod; 3. neck] • **Say:** *Point to row 4. Circle the word that has the same* *ending* *sound as dim.* Repeat for row 5. [5. bun]	1. write 2. knit 3. gnat 4. lamb 5. sign
68	**Say:** *Point to row 1. I am going to say a word. Find and circle the word in the row: wrap.* Repeat for rows 2–5. [2. knot; 3. limb; 4. gnome; 5. climb]	1. wrap 2. knot 3. limb 4. gnome 5. climb
69	**Say:** *Point to the picture in row 1. It is a picture of a pan. Circle the word that has the same /a/ sound as pan.* Repeat for rows 2–5. [2. bat; 3. hat; 4. jam; 5. bag]	1. sat 2. has 3. at 4. have 5. can
70	**Say:** *Point to the picture in row 1. It is a picture of a map. Circle the word that has the same /a/ sound as map.* Repeat for rows 2–5. [2. fan; 3. tack; 4. ham; 5. van]	1. pat 2. bad 3. ran 4. tan 5. sap
71	**Say:** *Point to the picture in row 1. It is a picture of a pin. Circle the word that has the same /i/ sound as pin.* Repeat for rows 2–5. [2. wig; 3. bib; 4. ship; 5. fin (picture of a shark, with an arrow pointing to the fin)]	1. big 2. him 3. nip 4. hid 5. sit
72	**Say:** *Point to the picture in row 1. It is a picture of a pig. Circle the word that has the same /i/ sound as pig.* Repeat for rows 2–5. [2. hill; 3. six; 4. lip; 5. kick (picture of a boy kicking a ball)]	1. fix 2. dig 3. bid 4. pin 5. jib
73	**Say:** *Point to the picture in row 1. It is a picture of a mop. Circle the word that has the same /o/ sound as mop.* Repeat for rows 2–5. [2. sock; 3. pot; 4. log; 5. box]	1. hot 2. top 3. sod 4. cot 5. lot
74	**Say:** *Point to the picture in row 1. It is a picture of a rock. Circle the word that has the same /o/ sound as rock.* Repeat for rows 2–5. [2. fox; 3. knot; 4. dog; 5. dot]	1. lock 2. rot 3. on 4. not 5. cob
75	**Say:** *Point to the picture in row 1. It is a picture of a bug. Circle the word that has the same /u/ sound as bug.* Repeat for rows 2–5. [2. sun; 3. cup; 4. bus; 5. duck]	1. sub 2. hut 3. gut 4. nut 5. mud
76	**Say:** *Point to row 1. I am going to say a word. Find and circle the word in the row: jug.* Repeat for rows 2–5. [2. cub; 3. luck; 4. run; 5. but]	1. jug 2. cub 3. luck 4. run 5. but
77	**Say:** *Point to the picture in row 1. It is a picture of a bed. Circle the word that has the same /e/ sound as bed.* Repeat for rows 2–5. [2. ten; 3. net; 4. vest; 5. web]	1. jet 2. went 3. deck 4. get 5. sell
78	**Say:** *Point to row 1. I am going to say a word. Find and circle the word in the row: red.* Repeat for rows 2–5. [2. den; 3. bet; 4. well; 5. men]	1. red 2. den 3. bet 4. well 5. men

Quick Check	Directions	Answers
79	**Say:** *Point to the picture in row 1. It is a picture of a rake. Circle the word that has the same /ā/ sound as rake.* Repeat for rows 2–5. [2. cape; 3. gate; 4. base; 5. lace]	1. made 2. tame 3. lake 4. rate 5. pane
80	**Say:** *Point to row 1. I am going to say a word. Find and circle the word in the row: late.* Repeat for rows 2–5. [2. tape; 3. sale; 4. cane; 5. bake]	1. late 2. tape 3. sale 4. cane 5. bake
81	**Say:** *Point to the picture in row 1. It is a picture of a bone. Circle the word that has the same /ō/ sound as bone.* Repeat for rows 2–5. [2. rope; 3. hose; 4. note; 5. pole (picture of a flag, with an arrow pointing to the pole)]	1. mole 2. woke 3. dome 4. hope 5. vote
82	**Say:** *Point to row 1. I am going to say a word. Find and circle the word in the row: cone.* Repeat for rows 2–5. [2. robe; 3. hope; 4. joke; 5. sole]	1. cone 2. robe 3. hope 4. joke 5. sole
83	**Say:** *Point to the picture in row 1. It is a picture of the number nine. Circle the word that has the same /ī/ sound as nine.* Repeat for rows 2–5. [2. slide; 3. bike; 4. dime; 5. kite]	1. ripe 2. mite 3. line 4. tile 5. wide
84	**Say:** *Point to row 1. I am going to say a word. Find and circle the word in the row: time.* Repeat for rows 2–5. [2. pile; 3. like; 4. side; 5. mine]	1. time 2. pile 3. like 4. side 5. mine
85	**Say:** *Point to the picture in row 1. It is a picture of a flute. Circle the word that has the same /ū/ sound as flute.* Repeat for rows 2–5. [2. cube; 3. mule; 4. prune; 5. tube]	1. rude 2. fuse 3. tune 4. dude 5. rule
86	**Say:** *Point to row 1. I am going to say a word. Find and circle the word in the row: cute.* Repeat for rows 2–5. [2. fume; 3. June; 4. tube; 5. mute]	1. cute 2. fume 3. June 4. tube 5. mute
87	**Say:** *Point to row 1. Circle the word that has the same /ā/ sound as date.* Repeat for rows 2–5. [2. name; 3. hail; 4. stay; 5. great]	1. sail 2. break 3. way 4. lake 5. tail
88	**Say:** *Point to row 1. I am going to say a word. Find and circle the word in the row: raid.* Repeat for rows 2–5. [2. may; 3. tape; 4. wait; 5. great]	1. raid 2. may 3. tape 4. wait 5. great
89	**Say:** *Point to row 1. Circle the word that has the same /ō/ sound as go.* Repeat for rows 2–5. [2. soap; 3. low; 4. toe; 5. coal]	1. tow 2. crow 3. float 4. road 5. no
90	**Say:** *Point to row 1. I am going to say a word. Find and circle the word in the row: load.* Repeat for rows 2–5. [2. bowl; 3. goes; 4. so; 5. grow]	1. load 2. bowl 3. goes 4. so 5. grow
91	**Say:** *Point to row 1. Circle the word that has the same /ē/ sound as see.* Repeat for rows 2–5. [2. tea; 3. thief; 4. he; 5. scene]	1. these 2. we 3. feel 4. bead 5. piece

Grades K–2
Teacher Administration and Answers

Quick Check	Directions	Answers	
92	**Say:** *Point to row 1. I am going to say a word. Find and circle the word in the row: sheet.* Repeat for rows 2–5. [2. beak; 3. theme; 4. me; 5. field]	1. sheet 2. beak 3. theme	4. me 5. field
93	**Say:** *Point to row 1. Circle the word that has the same /ē/ sound as money.* Repeat for rows 2–5. [2. honey 3. puppy; 4. valley; 5. city]	1. sea 2. key 3. we	4. leak 5. feed
94	**Say:** *Point to row 1. I am going to say a word. Find and circle the word in the row: funny.* Repeat for rows 2–5. [2. turkey; 3. jelly; 4. alley; 5. shiny]	1. funny 2. turkey 3. jelly	4. alley 5. shiny
95	**Say:** *Point to row 1. Circle the word that has the same /ī/ sound as pie.* Repeat for rows 2–5. [2. time 3. fly; 4. ice; 5. high]	1. my 2. sight 3. lie	4. fight 5. why
96	**Say:** *Point to row 1. I am going to say a word. Find and circle the word in the row: by.* Repeat for rows 2–5. [2. might; 3. tie; 4. hi; 5. sigh]	1. by 2. might 3. tie	4. hi 5. sigh
97	**Say:** *Point to row 1. Circle the word that has the same /ū/ sound as rule.* Repeat for rows 2–5. [2. stew; 3. tune; 4. glue; 5. huge]	1. due 2. clue 3. knew	4. blew 5. few
98	**Say:** *Point to row 1. I am going to say a word. Find and circle the word in the row: sue.* Repeat for rows 2–5. [2. flu; 3. true; 4. grew; 5. hew]	1. sue 2. flu 3. true	4. grew 5. hew
99	**Say:** *Point to the picture of row 1. It is a picture of a farm. Circle the word that has the same /är/ sound as farm.* Repeat for rows 2–5. [2. yard; 3. jar; 4. star; 5. shark]	1. cart 2. far 3. park	4. harm 5. barn
100	**Say:** *Point to row 1. I am going to say a word. Find and circle the word in the row: hard.* Repeat for rows 2–5. [2. sharp; 3. part; 4. tar; 5. mark]	1. hard 2. sharp 3. part	4. tar 5. mark
101	**Say:** *Point to the picture in row 1. It is a picture of corn. Circle the word that has the same /ôr/ sound as corn.* Repeat for rows 2–5. [2. soar; 3. horn; 4. shore; 5. horse]	1. tore 2. for 3. oar	4. born 5. core
102	**Say:** *Point to row 1. I am going to say a word. Find and circle the word in the row: more.* Repeat for rows 2–5. [2. cord; 3. roar; 4. torn; 5. score]	1. more 2. cord 3. roar	4. torn 5. score
103	**Say:** *Point to the picture in row 1. It is a picture of a person's hand stirring something. Circle the word that has the same /ûr/ sound as stir.* Repeat for rows 2–5. [2. curb; 3. fern; 4. spur; 5. girl]	1. curl 2. fur 3. turn	4. bird 5. hurt
104	**Say:** *Point to row 1. I am going to say a word. Find and circle the word in the row: nurse.* Repeat for rows 2–5. [2. were; 3. shirt; 4. burn; 5. dirt]	1. nurse 2. were 3. shirt	4. burn 5. dirt

Quick Check	Directions	Answers
105	**Say:** *Point to the picture in row 1. It is a picture of a deer. Circle the word that has the same /ir/ sound as deer.* Repeat for rows 2–5. [2. shear (picture of a sheep being sheared); 3. steer; 4. tear; 5. ear (picture of a boy, with an arrow pointing to his ear)]	1. near 2. peer 3. fear 4. here 5. rear
106	**Say:** *Point to row 1. I am going to say a word. Find and circle the word in the row: cheer.* Repeat for rows 2–5. [2. gear; 3. year; 4. smear; 5. mere]	1. cheer 2. gear 3. year 4. smear 5. mere
107	**Say:** *Point to the picture in row 1. It is a picture of a chair. Circle the word that has the same /âr/ sound as chair.* Repeat for rows 2–5. [2. square; 3. hair (picture of a girl, with an arrow pointing to her hair); 4. bear; 5. fair]	1. dare 2. pair 3. care 4. stair 5. wear
108	**Say:** *Point to row 1. I am going to say a word. Find and circle the word in the row: share.* Repeat for rows 2–5. [2. bare; 3. there; 4. hair; 5. mare]	1. share 2. bare 3. there 4. hair 5. mare
109	**Say:** *Point to the picture in row 1. It is a picture of a crown. Circle the word that has the same /ou/ sound as crown.* Repeat for rows 2–5. [2. house; 3. cloud; 4. cow; 5. mouse]	1. now 2. town 3. shout 4. loud 5. brown
110	**Say:** *Point to row 1. I am going to say a word. Find and circle the word in the row: found.* Repeat for rows 2–5. [2. down; 3. ground; 4. howl; 5. pout]	1. found 2. down 3. ground 4. howl 5. pout
111	**Say:** *Point to the picture in row 1. It is a picture of a coin. Circle the word that has the same /oi/ sound as coin.* Repeat for rows 2–5. [2. boy; 3. oil; 4. toy; 5. soil]	1. soy 2. point 3. noise 4. coil 5. foil
112	**Say:** *Point to row 1. I am going to say a word. Find and circle the word in the row: join.* Repeat for rows 2–5. [2. boil; 3. voice; 4. joy; 5. Roy]	1. join 2. boil 3. voice 4. joy 5. Roy
113	**Say:** *Point to the picture in row 1. It is a picture of tools. Circle the word that has the same /ū/ sound as tools.* Repeat for rows 2–5. [2. boot; 3. juice; 4. school; 5. moon]	1. soon 2. food 3. pool 4. soup 5. shoe
114	**Say:** *Point to row 1. I am going to say a word. Find and circle the word in the row: loop.* Repeat for rows 2–5. [2. stool; 3. group; 4. build; 5. you]	1. loop 2. stool 3. group 4. build 5. you
115	**Say:** *Point to the picture in row 1. It is a picture of a hook. Circle the word that has the same /o͝o/ sound as hook.* Repeat for rows 2–5. [2. wood; 3. brook; 4. hoof; 5. hood]	1. would 2. shook 3. foot 4. look 5. book
116	**Say:** *Point to row 1. I am going to say a word. Find and circle the word in the row: took.* Repeat for rows 2–5. [2. stood; 3. could; 4. wool; 5. foot]	1. took 2. stood 3. could 4. wool 5. foot

Grades K-2

Teacher Administration and Answers

Quick Check	Directions	Answers	
117	**Say:** *Point to the picture in row 1. It is a picture of a dog, with an arrow pointing to the paw. Circle the word that has the same /ŏ/ sound as paw.* Repeat for rows 2–5. [2. mall; 3. hall; 4. straw; 5. hawk]	1. haul 2. flaw 3. lawn	4. ball 5. fault
118	**Say:** *Point to row 1. I am going to say a word. Find and circle the word in the row: tall.* Repeat for rows 2–5. [2. claw; 3. caught; 4. launch; 5. walk]	1. tall 2. claw 3. caught	4. launch 5. walk
119	**Say:** *Read each sentence. On the line, write the contraction for the underlined words.*	1. doesn't 2. can't 3. hasn't	4. isn't 5. won't
120	**Say:** *Read each sentence and the three bold words below the sentence. Circle the word that best fits in the blank.*	1. weren't 2. couldn't 3. won't	4. doesn't 5. isn't
121	**Say:** *Read each sentence. On the line, write the contraction for the underlined words.*	1. You're 2. He's 3. Who's	4. What're 5. Here's
122	**Say:** *Read each sentence and the three bold words below the sentence. Circle the word that best fits in the blank.*	1. You're 2. it's 3. she's	4. We're 5. There's
123	**Say:** *Read each sentence. On the line, write the contraction for the underlined words.*	1. I'll 2. We've 3. They'll	4. I'm 5. You've
124	**Say:** *Read each sentence and the three bold words below the sentence. Circle the form of the word that best fits in the blank.*	1. I'm 2. She'll 3. They'll	4. I've 5. We've
125	**Say:** *Read each sentence. On the line, write the two words that make up the underlined compound word.*	1. book case 2. air port 3. some thing	4. home made 5. with out
126	**Say:** *Read each sentence and the three bold words below the sentence. Circle the word that best fits in the blank to complete the compound word.*	1. where 2. Some 3. every	4. one 5. noon
127	**Say:** *Read each sentence and the three bold words below the sentence. Circle the form of the word that best fits in the blank.*	1. foxes 2. boys 3. dishes	4. chairs 5. peaches
128	**Say:** *Read each sentence. On the line, write the plural form of the bold word.*	1. wishes 2. benches 3. boxes	4. chips 5. moths
129	**Say:** *Read each sentence and the three bold words below the sentence. Circle the form of the word that best fits in the blank.*	1. geese 2. mice 3. teeth	4. sheep 5. children
130	**Say:** *Read each sentence. On the line, write the plural form of the bold word.*	1. men 2. shelves 3. feet	4. leaves 5. wolves

Quick Check	Directions	Answers	
131	**Say:** *Read each sentence and the three bold words below the sentence. Circle the form of the word that best fits in the blank.*	1. wants 2. jumped 3. cleans	4. sailed 5. peeking
132	**Say:** *Read each sentence. Using one of the inflectional endings* -s, -ed, *or* -ing, *write the correct form of the bold word on the line.*	1. knows 2. floating 3. speaking	4. shouts 5. walked
133	**Say:** *Read each sentence and the three bold words below each sentence. Circle the form of the word that best fits in the blank.*	1. skipped 2. riding 3. stopped	4. waving 5. jogging
134	**Say:** *Read each sentence. Using the inflectional ending* -ed *or* -ing, *write the correct form of the bold word on the line.*	1. smiling 2. clapped 3. sitting	4. planned 5. writing
135	**Say:** *Read each sentence and the three bold words below the sentence. Circle the form of the word that best fits in the blank.*	1. cries 2. stories 3. libraries	4. puppies 5. spies
136	**Say:** *Read each sentence. Using the inflectional ending* -es, *write the correct form of the bold word on the line.*	1. berries 2. ladies 3. pennies	4. ponies 5. daisies
137	**Say:** *Read each sentence and the three bold words below the sentence. Circle the form of the word that best fits in the blank.*	1. smallest 2. taller 3. prettiest	4. biggest 5. softer
138	**Say:** *Read each sentence. Using the comparative inflectional ending* -er *or* -est, *write the correct form of the bold word on the line.*	1. fastest 2. sharper 3. shiniest	4. lighter 5. happiest
139	**Say:** *Read each sentence and the three bold words below the sentence. Circle the form of the word that best fits in the blank.*	1. girl's 2. children's 3. swings'	4. dog's 5. family's
140	**Say:** *Read each sentence. On the line, write the possessive form of the bold word.*	1. cars' 2. sister's 3. friends'	4. boy's 5. truck's
141	**Say:** *Point to row 1. I'm going to read each word aloud. After I read the word, draw a line to divide the word into syllables: napkin, dentist.* Repeat for rows 2–5. [2. sunset, pumpkin; 3. pencil, contest; 4. rubber, until; 5. cobweb, bedbug]	1. nap|kin 2. sun|set 3. pen|cil 4. rub|ber 5. cob|web	den|tist pump|kin con|test un|til bed|bug
142	**Say:** *Point to row 1. I'm going to read each word aloud. After I read the word, draw a line to divide the word into syllables: button, cannot.* Repeat for rows 2–5. [2. insect, cactus; 3. sudden, himself; 4. pennies, happen; 5. subway, kitten]	1. but|ton 2. in|sect 3. sud|den 4. pen|nies 5. sub|way	can|not cac|tus him|self hap|pen kit|ten
143	**Say:** *Point to row 1. I'm going to read each word aloud. After I read the word, draw a line to divide the word into syllables: admire, sunrise.* Repeat for rows 2–5. [2. explode, costume; 3. inside, tadpole; 4. excuse, nickname; 5. conclude, pancake]	1. ad|mire 2. ex|plode 3. in|side 4. ex|cuse 5. con|clude	sun|rise cos|tume tad|pole nick|name pan|cake

Grades K-2

Teacher Administration and Answers

<table>
<tr><th>Quick Check</th><th>Directions</th><th>Answers</th><th></th></tr>
<tr><td>144</td><td>Say: Point to row 1. I'm going to read each word aloud. After I read the word, draw a line to divide the word into syllables: mistake, suppose. Repeat for rows 2–5. [2. beware, bedtime; 3. homemade, include; 4. decide, compare; 5. mistake, someplace]</td><td>1. mis|take
2. be|ware
3. home|made
4. de|cide
5. mi|stake</td><td>sup|pose
bed|time
in|clude
com|pare
some|place</td></tr>
<tr><td>145</td><td>Say: Point to row 1. I'm going to read each word aloud. After I read the word, draw a line to divide the word into syllables: baby, open. Repeat for rows 2–5. [2. spider, table; 3. paper, moment; 4. silent, pony; 5. music, remind]</td><td>1. ba|by
2. spi|der
3. pa|per
4. si|lent
5. mu|sic</td><td>o|pen
ta|ble
mo|ment
po|ny
re|mind</td></tr>
<tr><td>146</td><td>Say: Point to row 1. I'm going to read each word aloud. After I read the word, draw a line to divide the word into syllables: solo, wavy. Repeat for rows 2–5. [2. rotate, remove; 3. label, item; 4. human, motor; 5. notice, zero]</td><td>1. so|lo
2. ro|tate
3. la|bel
4. hu|man
5. no|tice</td><td>wa|vy
re|move
i|tem
mo|tor
ze|ro</td></tr>
<tr><td>147</td><td>Say: Point to row 1. I'm going to read each word aloud. After I read the word, draw a line to divide the word into syllables: perform, urgent.
Repeat for rows 2–5. [2. forest, turnip; 3. stairway, berry; 4. thunder, nursing; 5. fairness, artist]</td><td>1. per|form
2. for|est
3. stair|way
4. thun|der
5. fair|ness</td><td>ur|gent
tur|nip
ber|ry
nurs|ing
art|ist</td></tr>
<tr><td>148</td><td>Say: Point to row 1. I'm going to read each word aloud. After I read the word, draw a line to divide the word into syllables: order, birthday. Repeat for rows 2–5. [2. marble, thirsty; 3. surfer, forty; 4. purple, turkey; 5. explore, perfect]</td><td>1. or|der
2. mar|ble
3. surf|er
4. purp|le
5. ex|plore</td><td>birth|day
thirst|y
for|ty
tur|key
per|fect</td></tr>
<tr><td>149</td><td>Say: Point to row 1. I'm going to read each word aloud. After I read the word, draw a line to divide the word into syllables: detail, rowboat. Repeat for rows 2–5. [2. money, teacher; 3. playmate, foamy; 4. easy, between; 5. lookout, untie]</td><td>1. de|tail
2. mon|ey
3. play|mate
4. eas|y
5. look|out</td><td>row|boat
teach|er
foam|y
be|tween
un|tie</td></tr>
<tr><td>150</td><td>Say: Point to row 1. I'm going to read each word aloud. After I read the word, draw a line to divide the word into syllables: valley, delight. Repeat for rows 2–5. [2. hockey, mailbox; 3. eighty, below; 4. relieve, people; 5. roadway, haystack]</td><td>1. val|ley
2. hock|ey
3. eight|y
4. re|lieve
5. road|way</td><td>de|light
mail|box
be|low
peo|ple
hay|stack</td></tr>
<tr><td>151</td><td>Say: Point to row 1. I'm going to read each word aloud. After I read the word, draw a line to divide the word into syllables: paddle, buckle. Repeat for rows 2–5. [2. apple, settle; 3. juggle, circle; 4. rumble, sparkle; 5. tangle, cable]</td><td>1. pad|dle
2. ap|ple
3. jug|gle
4. rum|ble
5. tan|gle</td><td>buck|le
set|tle
cir|cle
spar|kle
ca|ble</td></tr>
<tr><td>152</td><td>Say: Point to row 1. I'm going to read each word aloud. After I read the word, draw a line to divide the word into syllables: eagle, pickle. Repeat for rows 2–5. [2. huddle, little; 3. table, ankle; 4. single, tumble; 5. bottle, bugle]</td><td>1. ea|gle
2. hud|dle
3. ta|ble
4. sin|gle
5. bot|tle</td><td>pick|le
lit|tle
an|kle
tum|ble
bu|gle</td></tr>
<tr><td>153</td><td>Say: Read each sentence. On the line, write the correct prefix from the box to complete the word in the sentence.</td><td>1. re
2. dis
3. un</td><td>4. dis
5. un
6. re</td></tr>
</table>

Quick Check	Directions	Answers
154	**Say:** *Read each sentence and the three bold prefixes below the sentence. Circle the prefix that best fits in the blank to complete the word in the sentence.*	1. un- 2. dis- 3. re- 4. dis- 5. re- 6. un-
155	**Say:** *Read each sentence. On the line, write the correct ending from the box to complete the word in the sentence.*	1. er 2. or 3. or 4. er 5. er 6. or
156	**Say:** *Read each sentence and the two bold endings below the sentence. Circle the ending that best fits in the blank to complete the word in the sentence.*	1. -er 2. -or 3. -er 4. -er 5. -or 6. -or
157	**Say:** *Read each sentence. On the line, write the correct ending from the box to complete the word in the sentence.*	1. y 2. ly 3. ly 4. y 5. ly 6. y
158	**Say:** *Read each sentence and the two bold endings below the sentence. Circle the ending that best fits in the blank to complete the word in the sentence.*	1. -y 2. -ly 3. -ly 4. -y 5. -ly 6. -y
159	**Say:** *Read each sentence. On the line, write the correct suffix from the box to complete the word in the sentence.*	1. ful 2. ful 3. ful 4. less 5. ful 6. less
160	**Say:** *Read each sentence and the two bold suffixes below the sentence. Circle the suffix that best fits in the blank to complete the word in the sentence.*	1. -less 2. -ful 3. -less 4. -ful 5. -less 6. -ful
161	**Say:** *Point to row 1. Say the words in the row.* Repeat for row 2. Use the Answers column to follow along as the student reads. Mark correct and incorrect answers on the student's paper per row.	1. we, like, the 2. see, I, go
162	**Say:** *Point to row 1. Say the words in the row.* Repeat for rows 2–4. Use the Answers column to follow along as the student reads. Mark correct and incorrect answers on the student's paper per row.	1. the, we, see 2. go, she, can 3. is, a, he 4. has, play, little
163	**Say:** *Point to row 1. Say the words in the row.* Repeat for rows 2–4. Use the Answers column to follow along as the student reads. Mark correct and incorrect answers on the student's paper per row.	1. he, has, play 2. little, and, you 3. with, big, for 4. no, jump, one
164	**Say:** *Point to row 1. Say the words in the row.* Repeat for rows 2–4. Use the Answers column to follow along as the student reads. Mark correct and incorrect answers on the student's paper per row.	1. for, no, jump 2. one, have, are 3. said, two, look 4. me, come, here
165	**Say:** *Point to row 1. Say the words in the row.* Repeat for rows 2–4. Use the Answers column to follow along as the student reads. Mark correct and incorrect answers on the student's paper per row.	1. look, me, come 2. here, to, my 3. of, what, put 4. want, this, saw

Grades K-2
Teacher Administration and Answers

Quick Check	Directions	Answers
166	**Say:** *Point to row 1. Say the words in the row.* Repeat for rows 2–13. Use the Answers column to follow along as the student reads. Mark correct and incorrect answers on the student's paper per row.	1. I, like, the 2. we, see, go 3. she, can, is 4. a, he, has 5. play, little, and 6. you, with, big 7. for, no, jump 8. one, have, are 9. said, two, look 10. me, come, here 11. to, my, of 12. what, put, want 13. this, saw
167	**Say:** *Point to row 1. Say the words in the row.* Repeat for rows 2–5. Use the Answers column to follow along as the student reads. Mark correct and incorrect answers on the student's paper per row.	1. the, see, go 2. she, and, play 3. little, you, with 4. for, no, jump 5. one, have
168	**Say:** *Point to row 1. Say the words in the row.* Repeat for rows 2–5. Use the Answers column to follow along as the student reads. Mark correct and incorrect answers on the student's paper per row.	1. are, said, two 2. look, me, come 3. here, to, my 4. of, what, put 5. want, this, saw
169	**Say:** *Point to row 1. Say the words in the row.* Repeat for rows 2–4. Use the Answers column to follow along as the student reads. Mark correct and incorrect answers on the student's paper per row.	1. now, do, which 2. went, was, there 3. then, out, who 4. good, by, them
170	**Say:** *Point to row 1. Say the words in the row.* Repeat for rows 2–4. Use the Answers column to follow along as the student reads. Mark correct and incorrect answers on the student's paper per row.	1. were, our, could 2. these, once, upon 3. hurt, that, because 4. from, their, when
171	**Say:** *Point to row 1. Say the words in the row.* Repeat for rows 2–4. Use the Answers column to follow along as the student reads. Mark correct and incorrect answers on the student's paper per row.	1. why, many, right 2. start, find, how 3. over, under, try 4. give, far, too
172	**Say:** *Point to row 1. Say the words in the row.* Repeat for rows 2–4. Use the Answers column to follow along as the student reads. Mark correct and incorrect answers on the student's paper per row.	1. after, call, large 2. her, house, long 3. off, small, brown 4. work, year, live
173	**Say:** *Point to row 1. Say the words in the row.* Repeat for rows 2–4. Use the Answers column to follow along as the student reads. Mark correct and incorrect answers on the student's paper per row.	1. found, your, know 2. always, all, people 3. where, draw, again 4. round, they, country

Quick Check	Directions	Answers
174	**Say:** *Point to row 1. Say the words in the row.* Repeat for rows 2–4. Use the Answers column to follow along as the student reads. Mark correct and incorrect answers on the student's paper per row.	1. four, great, boy 2. city, laugh, move 3. change, away, every 4. near, school, earth
175	**Say:** *Point to row 1. Say the words in the row.* Repeat for rows 2–4. Use the Answers column to follow along as the student reads. Mark correct and incorrect answers on the student's paper per row.	1. before, done, about 2. even, walk, buy 3. only, through, does 4. another, wash, some
176	**Say:** *Point to row 1. Say the words in the row.* Repeat for rows 2–4. Use the Answers column to follow along as the student reads. Mark correct and incorrect answers on the student's paper per row.	1. better, carry, learn 2. very, mother, father 3. never, below, blue 4. answer, eight, any
177	**Say:** *Point to row 1. Say the words in the row.* Repeat for rows 2–10. Use the Answers column to follow along as the student reads. Mark correct and incorrect answers on the student's paper per row.	1. a, can, and 2. come, are, for 3. big, go, has 4. I, have, is 5. jump, my, one 6. put, the, want 7. what, you, he 8. like, little, no 9. of, saw, this 10. to, we, with
178	**Say:** *Point to row 1. Say the words in the row.* Repeat for rows 2–10. Use the Answers column to follow along as the student reads. Mark correct and incorrect answers on the student's paper per row.	1. here, look, me 2. play, said, see 3. she, try, about 4. because, after, before 5. call, do, earth 6. father, give, her 7. know, large, many 8. near, off, people 9. right, school, that 10. two, under, very
179	**Say:** *Point to row 1. Say the words in the row.* Repeat for rows 2–10. Use the Answers column to follow along as the student reads. Mark correct and incorrect answers on the student's paper per row.	1. again, below, carry 2. does, eight, find 3. good, house, laugh 4. mother, move, never 5. once, round, small 6. their, too, walk 7. where, year, all 8. away, better, by 9. change, done, even 10. found, learn, only
180	**Say:** *Point to row 1. Say the words in the row.* Repeat for rows 2–10. Use the Answers column to follow along as the student reads. Mark correct and incorrect answers on the student's paper per row.	1. long, now, our 2. some, them, through 3. upon, was, when 4. work, always, any 5. blue, buy, city 6. draw, four, great 7. how, live, another 8. boy, could, every 9. far, from, hurt 10. over, out, these
181	**Say:** *Point to row 1. Say the words in the row.* Repeat for rows 2–10. Use the Answers column to follow along as the student reads. Mark correct and incorrect answers on the student's paper per row.	1. answer, brown, country 2. start, then, there 3. wash, went, who 4. your, above, began 5. different, enough, few 6. grow, they, were 7. which, why, follow 8. girl, head, idea 9. kind, leave, might 10. next, often, paper
182	**Say:** *Point to row 1. Say the words in the row.* Repeat for rows 2–10. Use the Answers column to follow along as the student reads. Mark correct and incorrect answers on the student's paper per row.	1. point, river, second 2. song, think, three 3. until, watch, white 4. young, add, between 5. close, example, food 6. group, hear, home 7. left, mountain, music 8. night, old, picture 9. sentence, spell, thought 10. together, while, world

Grades K-2

Teacher Administration and Answers

Quick Check	Directions	Answers	
183	**Say:** *Point to row 1. Say the words in the row.* Repeat for rows 2–10. Use the Answers column to follow along as the student reads. Mark correct and incorrect answers on the student's paper per row.	1. air, along, begin 2. children, important, letter 3. open, own, sound 4. talk, almost, animal 5. around, body, color	6. eye, form, high 7. light, story, across 8. become, complete, during 9. happened, hundred, problem 10. toward, study, wind
184	**Say:** *Point to row 1. Say the words in the row.* Repeat for rows 2–10. Use the Answers column to follow along as the student reads. Mark correct and incorrect answers on the student's paper per row.	1. against, certain, door 2. early, field, heard 3. knew, listen, morning 4. several, area, ever 5. hours, measure, notice	6. order, piece, short 7. today, true, covered 8. cried, figure, horse 9. money, products, question 10. since, usually, voice
185	**Say:** *Point to row 1. Say the words in the row.* Repeat for rows 2–10. Use the Answers column to follow along as the student reads. Mark correct and incorrect answers on the student's paper per row.	1. able, behind, carefully 2. common, easy, fact 3. remember, sure, vowel 4. whole, ago, government 5. half, machine, pair	6. quickly, scientist, thousand 7. understood, wait, among 8. building, circle, decided 9. finally, heavy, include 10. nothing, special, wheel
186	**Say:** *Point to row 1. Say the words in the row.* Repeat for rows 2–10. Use the Answers column to follow along as the student reads. Mark correct and incorrect answers on the student's paper per row.	1. brought, contain, front 2. gave, inches, material 3. noun, ocean, strong 4. verb, built, correct 5. inside, island, language	6. oh, person, street 7. system, warm, dark 8. clear, explain, force 9. minutes, object, plane 10. power, produce, surface

Grades K–2

Quick Check to Intervention Resource Map

Skill	Quick Check	*Benchmark Advance* PWR Intervention Lessons	Page
Letter Identification	1 (p. 2) 2 (p. 3)	See *Benchmark Advance Print Concepts* Intervention **Grade K** Lesson 7: Recognize and Name all Uppercase and Lowercase Letters of the alphabet	14
		See *Benchmark Advance Print Concepts* Intervention **Grade 1** Lesson 9: Recognize and Name all Uppercase and Lowercase Letters of the alphabet	18
		See *Benchmark Advance Print Concepts* Intervention **Grade 2** Lesson 9: Recognize and Name all Uppercase and Lowercase Letters of the Alphabet	18
Initial and Final Consonant *m*	3 (p. 4) 4 (p. 5)	**Grade K** Lesson 1: Initial Consonant *Mm*	2
		Lesson 21: Final Consonant *Mm*	42
		Grade 1 Lesson 41: Initial Consonant *Mm*	82
		Lesson 61: Final Consonant *Mm*	122
		Grade 2 Lesson 76: Initial Consonant *Mm*	152
		Lesson 96: Final Consonant *Mm*	192
Initial and Final Consonant *t*	5 (p. 6) 6 (p. 7)	**Grade K** Lesson 3: Initial Consonant *Tt*	6
		Lesson 22: Final Consonant *Tt*	44
		Grade 1 Lesson 43: Initial Consonant *Tt*	86
		Lesson 62: Final Consonant *Tt*	124
		Grade 2 Lesson 78: Initial Consonant *Tt*	156
		Lesson 97: Final Consonant *Tt*	194
Initial and Final Consonant *n*	7 (p. 8) 8 (p. 9)	**Grade K** Lesson 4: Initial Consonant *Nn*	8
		Lesson 23: Final Consonant *Nn*	47
		Grade 1 Lesson 44: Initial Consonant *Nn*	88
		Lesson 63: Final Consonant *Nn*	127
		Grade 2 Lesson 79: Initial Consonant *Nn*	158
		Lesson 98: Final Consonant *Nn*	196

Skill	Quick Check	*Benchmark Advance* **PWR Intervention Lessons**	Page
Initial and Final Consonant *p*	9 (p. 10) 10 (p. 11)	**Grade K** Lesson 6: Initial Consonant *Pp* Lesson 24: Final Consonant *Pp*	12 48
		Grade 1 Lesson 46: Initial Consonant *Pp* Lesson 64: Final Consonant *Pp*	92 128
		Grade 2 Lesson 81: Initial Consonant *Pp* Lesson 99: Final Consonant *Pp*	162 198
Initial and Final Consonant *b*	11 (p. 12) 12 (p. 13)	**Grade K** Lesson 9: Initial Consonant *Bb* Lesson 25: Final Consonant *Bb*	18 50
		Grade 1: Lesson 49: Initial Consonant *Bb* Lesson 65: Final Consonant *Bb*	98 130
		Grade 2 Lesson 84: Initial Consonant *Bb* Lesson 100: Final Consonant *Bb*	168 200
Initial and Final Consonant *d*	13 (p. 14) 14 (p. 15)	**Grade K** Lesson 12: Initial Consonant *Dd* Lesson 27: Final Consonant *Dd*	24 54
		Grade 1 Lesson 52: Initial Consonant *Dd* Lesson 67: Final Consonant *Dd*	104 134
		Grade 2 Lesson 87: Initial Consonant *Dd* Lesson 102: Final Consonant *Dd*	174 204
Initial and Final Consonant *g*	15 (p. 16) 16 (p. 17)	**Grade K** Lesson 11: Initial Consonant *Gg* Lesson 26: Final Consonant *Gg*	22 52
		Grade 1 Lesson 51: Initial Consonant *Gg* Lesson 66: Final Consonant *Gg*	102 132
		Grade 2 Lesson 86: Initial Consonant *Gg* Lesson 101: Final Consonant *Gg*	172 202
Initial Consonant *s*	17 (p. 18) 18 (p. 19)	**Grade K** Lesson 2: Initial Consonant *Ss*	4
		Grade 1 Lesson 42: Initial Consonant *Ss*	84
		Grade 2 Lesson 77: Initial Consonant *Ss*	154

Grades K-2

Quick Check to Intervention Resource Map

Skill	Quick Check	*Benchmark Advance* PWR Intervention Lessons	Page
Initial Consonant *r*	19 (p. 20) 20 (p. 21)	**Grade K** Lesson 10: Initial Consonant *Rr*	20
		Grade 1 Lesson 50: Initial Consonant *Rr*	100
		Grade 2 Lesson 85: Initial Consonant *Rr*	170
Initial Consonant *f*	21 (p. 22) 22 (p. 23)	**Grade K** Lesson 5: Initial Consonant *Ff*	10
		Grade 1 Lesson 45: Initial Consonant *Ff*	90
		Grade 2 Lesson 80: Initial Consonant *Ff*	160
Initial Consonant *c* /k/	23 (p. 24) 24 (p. 25)	**Grade K** Lesson 7: Initial Consonant *Cc*	14
		Grade 1 Lesson 47: Initial Consonant *Cc*	94
		Grade 2 Lesson 82: Initial Consonant *Cc*	164
Initial Consonant *h*	25 (p. 26) 26 (p. 27)	**Grade K** Lesson 8: Initial Consonant *Hh*	16
		Grade 1 Lesson 48: Initial Consonant *Hh*	96
		Grade 2 Lesson 83: Initial Consonant *Hh*	166
Initial Consonant *w*	27 (p. 28) 28 (p. 29)	**Grade K** Lesson 13: Initial Consonant *Ww*	26
		Grade 1 Lesson 53: Initial Consonant *Ww*	106
		Grade 2 Lesson 88 Initial Consonant *Ww*	176
Initial Consonant *l*	29 (p. 30) 30 (p. 31)	**Grade K** Lesson 14: Initial Consonant *Ll*	28
		Grade 1 Lesson 54: Initial Consonant *Ll*	108
		Grade 2 Lesson 89: Initial Consonant *Ll*	178

Skill	**Quick Check**	***Benchmark Advance*** **PWR Intervention Lessons**	**Page**
Initial Consonant *j*	31 (p. 32) 32 (p. 33)	**Grade K** Lesson 15: Initial Consonant *Jj*	30
		Grade 1 Lesson 55: Initial Consonant *Jj*	110
		Grade 2 Lesson 90: Initial Consonant *Jj*	180
Initial Consonant *k*	33 (p. 32) 34 (p. 33)	**Grade K** Lesson 16: Initial Consonant *Kk*	32
		Grade 1 Lesson 56: Initial Consonant *Kk*	112
		Grade 2 Lesson 91: Initial Consonant *Kk*	182
Initial Consonant *y*	35 (p. 36) 36 (p. 37)	**Grade K** Lesson 17: Initial Consonant *Yy*	34
		Grade 1 Lesson 57: Initial Consonant *Yy*	114
		Grade 2 Lesson 92: Initial Consonant *Yy*	184
Initial Consonant *v*	37 (p. 38) 38 (p. 39)	**Grade K** Lesson 18: Initial Consonant *Vv*	36
		Grade 1 Lesson 58: Initial Consonant *Vv*	116
		Grade 2 Lesson 93: Initial Consonant *Vv*	186
Initial Consonant *qu*	39 (p. 40) 40 (p. 41)	**Grade K** Lesson 19: Initial Consonant *Qq*	38
		Grade 1 Lesson 59: Initial Consonant *Qq*	118
		Grade 2 Lesson 94: Initial Consonant *Qq*	188
Initial Consonant *z*	41 (p. 42) 42 (p. 43)	**Grade K** Lesson 20: Initial Consonant *Zz*	40
		Grade 1 Lesson 60: Initial Consonant *Zz*	120
		Grade 2 Lesson 95: Initial Consonant *Zz*	190

Grades K-2

Quick Check to Intervention Resource Map

Skill	Quick Check	*Benchmark Advance* **PWR Intervention Lessons**	Page
Final Consonant *x*	43 (p. 44) 44 (p. 45)	**Grade K** Lesson 28: Final Consonant *Xx*	56
		Grade 1 Lesson 68: Initial Consonant *Xx*	136
		Grade 2 Lesson 103: Initial Consonant *Xx*	206
Final Consonant *s* /z/	45 (p. 46) 46 (p. 47)	**Grade 1** Lesson 32: Read Nouns with Inflectional Ending: *-s* Lesson 33: Read Verbs with Inflectional Ending: *-s*	64 66
		Grade 2 Lesson 49: Identify and Name Inflectional Endings *-s, -ed, -ing*	98
Final Consonant *ck* /k/	47 (p. 48) 48 (p. 49)	**Grade 1** Lesson 6: Identify and Name Digraphs: *ck, ch, tch*	12
		Grade 2 Lesson 46: Identify and Name Digraphs: *ck, ch, tch*	92
Double Final Consonants	49 (p. 50) 50 (p. 51)	**Grade 1** Lesson 1: Identify and Name Double Final Consonants	2
		Grade 2 Lesson 41: Identify and Name Double Final Consonants	82
Consonant Blends (*l*-blends)	51 (p. 52) 52 (p. 53)	**Grade 1** Lesson 2: *L* Blends	4
		Grade 2 Lesson 42: *L* Blends	84
Consonant Blends (*s*-blends)	53 (p. 54) 54 (p. 55)	**Grade 1** Lesson 4: *S* Blends	8
		Grade 2 Lesson 44: *S* Blends	88
Consonant Blends (*r*-blends)	55 (p. 56) 56 (p. 57)	**Grade 1:** Lesson 3: *R* blends	6
		Grade 2: Lesson 43: *R* blends	86

Skill	Quick Check	*Benchmark Advance* PWR Intervention Lessons	Page
Three-Letter Blends	57 (p. 58) 58 (p. 59)	**Grade 1** Lesson 10: 3-letter blends: *scr, spr, spl, str*	20
		Grade 2 Lesson 52: 3-letter blends: *scr, spr, spl, str*	104
Final Consonant Blends	59 (p. 60) 60 (p. 61)	**Grade 1** Lesson 5: Final Blends	10
		Grade 2 Lesson 45: Final Blends	90
Consonant Digraphs (*th, sh, ng*)	61 (p. 62) 62 (p. 63)	**Grade 1** Lesson 7: Digraph: *sh* Lesson 8: Digraphs: *th, wh*	14 16
		Grade 2 Lesson 47: Digraph: *sh* Lesson 48: Digraphs: *th, wh*	94 96
Consonant Digraphs (*ch, tch, wh*)	63 (p. 64) 64 (p. 65)	**Grade 1** Lesson 6: Digraphs: *ck, ch, tch*	12
		Grade 2 Lesson 46: Digraphs: *ck, ch, tch*	92
Soft *c, g*	65 (p. 66) 66 (p. 67)	**Grade 1** Lesson 11: Soft *g, c*	22
		Grade 2 Lesson 53: Soft *g, c*	106
Silent Letters (*wr, kn, gn, mb*)	67 (p. 68) 68 (p. 69)	**Grade 1** Lesson 28: Silent Letters: *wr, kn, gn*	56
		Grade 2 Lesson 72: Silent Letters: *wr, kn, gn*	144
Short Vowel *a*	69 (p. 70) 70 (p. 71)	**Grade K** Lesson 29: Initial Short Vowel *a* **Grade K** Lesson 34: Medial Short Vowel *a*	58 68
		Grade 1 Lesson 69: Initial Short Vowel *a* **Grade 1** Lesson 74: Medial Short Vowel *a*	138 148
		Grade 2 Lesson 104: Initial Short Vowel *a* **Grade 2** Lesson 109: Medial Short Vowel *a*	208 218

Grades K-2

Quick Check to Intervention Resource Map

Skill	Quick Check	*Benchmark Advance* PWR Intervention Lessons	Page
Short Vowel *i*	71 (p. 72) 72 (p. 73)	**Grade K** Lesson 30: Initial Short Vowel *i* **Grade K** Lesson 35: Medial Short Vowel *i*	60 70
		Grade 1 Lesson 70: Initial Short Vowel *i* **Grade 1** Lesson 75: Medial Short Vowel *i*	140 150
		Grade 2 Lesson 105: Initial Short Vowel *i* **Grade 2** Lesson 110: Medial Short Vowel *i*	210 220
Short Vowel *o*	73 (p. 74) 74 (p. 75)	**Grade K** Lesson 31: Initial Short Vowel *o* **Grade K** Lesson 36: Medial Short Vowel *o*	62 72
		Grade 1 Lesson 71: Initial Short Vowel *o* **Grade 1** Lesson 76: Medial Short Vowel *o*	142 152
		Grade 2 Lesson 107: Initial Short Vowel *o* **Grade 2** Lesson 111: Medial Short Vowel *o*	214 222
Short Vowel *u*	75 (p. 76) 76 (p. 77)	**Grade K** Lesson 32: Initial Short Vowel *u* **Grade K** Lesson 37: Medial Short Vowel *u*	64 74
		Grade 1 Lesson 72: Initial Short Vowel *u* **Grade 1** Lesson 77: Medial Short Vowel *u*	144 154
		Grade 2 Lesson 107: Initial Short Vowel *u* **Grade 2** Lesson 112: Medial Short Vowel *u*	214 224
Short Vowel *e*	77 (p. 78) 78 (p. 79)	**Grade K** Lesson 33: Initial Short Vowel *e* **Grade K** Lesson 38: Medial Short Vowel *e*	66 76
		Grade 1 Lesson 73: Initial Short Vowel *e* **Grade 1** Lesson 78: Medial Short Vowel *e*	146 156
		Grade 2 Lesson 108: Initial Short Vowel *e* **Grade 2** Lesson 113: Medial Short Vowel *e*	216 226
Long Vowel *a* (*a_e*)	79 (p. 80) 80 (p. 81)	**Grade K** Lesson 44: Differentiate Between Long and Short Vowel *a*	88
		Grade 1 Lesson 84: Differentiate Between Long and Short Vowel *a*	168
		Grade 2 Lesson 119: Differentiate Between Long and Short Vowel *a*	238
Long Vowel *o* (*o_e*)	81 (p. 82) 82 (p. 83)	**Grade K** Lesson 46: Differentiate Between Long and Short Vowel *o*	92
		Grade 1 Lesson 86: Differentiate Between Long and Short Vowel *o*	172
		Grade 2 Lesson 121: Differentiate Between Long and Short Vowel *o*	242

Skill	Quick Check	*Benchmark Advance* PWR Intervention Lessons	Page
Long Vowel *i* (*i_e*)	83 (p. 84) 84 (p. 85)	**Grade K** Lesson 45: Differentiate Between Long and Short Vowel *i*	90
		Grade 1 Lesson 85: Differentiate Between Long and Short Vowel *i*	170
		Grade 2 Lesson 120: Differentiate Between Long and Short Vowel *i*	240
Long Vowel *u* (*u_e*)	85 (p. 86) 86 (p. 87)	**Grade K** Lesson 47: Differentiate Between Long and Short Vowel *u*	94
		Grade 1 Lesson 87: Differentiate Between Long and Short Vowel *u*	174
		Grade 2 Lesson 122: Differentiate Between Long and Short Vowel *u*	244
Long *a* Vowel Teams (*a, ai, ay, ea*)	87 (p. 88) 88 (p. 89)	**Grade 1** Lesson 17: Long *a*: *a, ai, ay*	34
		Grade 2 Lesson 60: Long *a*	120
Long *o* Vowel Teams and Single Letter (*o, oa, ow, oe*)	89 (p. 90) 90 (p. 91)	**Grade 1** Lesson 18: Long *o*: *o, oa, ow, oe*	36
		Grade 2 Lesson 61: Long *o*	122
Long *e* Vowel Teams and Single Letter (*e, ee, e_e, ea, ie*)	91 (p. 92) 92 (p. 93)	**Grade 1** Lesson 19: Long *e*: *e, ee, ea, ie*	38
		Grade 2 Lesson 62: Long *e*	124
Long *e* (*y, ey*)	93 (p. 94) 94 (p. 95)	**Grade 1** Lesson 30: Long *e* Sound: *y, ey*	60
		Grade 2 Lesson 74: Long *e*	148
Long *i* Vowel Teams and Single Letter (*i, ie, y, igh*)	95 (p. 96) 96 (p. 97)	**Grade 1** Lesson 20: Long *i*: *y, igh*	40
		Grade 2 Lesson 63: Long *i*	126
Long *u* Vowel Teams and Single Letter (*u, ew, ue*)	97 (p. 98) 98 (p. 99)	**Grade 2** Lesson 8: Long *u*	16

Grades K-2

Quick Check to Intervention Resource Map

Skill	Quick Check	*Benchmark Advance* PWR Intervention Lessons	Page
r-Controlled Vowels: /är/ (*ar*)	99 (p. 100) 100 (p. 101)	**Grade 1** Lesson 22: Identify and Name Variant Vowel: *är*	44
		Grade 2 Lesson 9: Identify and Name Variant Vowel: *är*	18
		Lesson 65: Identify and Name Variant Vowel: *är*	130
r-Controlled Vowels: /ôr/ (*or, oar, ore*)	101 (p. 102) 102 (p. 103)	**Grade 1** Lesson 23: Identify and Name Variant Vowel: *ôr*	46
		Grade 2 Lesson 12: Identify and Name Variant Vowel: *ôr*	24
		Lesson 66: Identify and Name Variant Vowel: *ôr*	132
r-Controlled Vowels: /ûr/ (*er, ir, ur*)	103 (p. 104) 104 (p. 105)	**Grade 1** Lesson 24: Identify and Name Variant Vowel: *ûr*	48
		Grade 2 Lesson 11: Identify and Name Variant Vowel: *ûr*	22
		Lesson 67: Identify and Name Variant Vowel: *ûr*	134
r-Controlled Vowels: /ir/ (*ear, eer, ere*)	105 (p. 106) 106 (p. 107)	**Grade 2** Lesson 13: Recognize *r*-Controlled Syllable Patterns with Long *Ee*	26
r-Controlled Vowels: /âr/ (*air, are, ear, ere*)	107 (p. 108) 108 (p. 109)	**Grade 2** Lesson 14: Recognize *r*-Controlled Syllable Patterns with Long *Aa*	28
Vowel-Sound /ou/ (*ou, ow*)	109 (p. 110) 110 (p. 111)	**Grade 1** Lesson 25: Identify and Name Vowel Team: *ou*	50
Vowel-Sound /oi/ (*oi, oy*)	111 (p. 112) 112 (p. 113)	**Grade 1** Lesson 26: Identify and Name Vowel Team: *oi*	52
Vowel Teams /ū/ (*oo, ou, ui, oe*)	113 (p. 114) 114 (p. 115)	**Grade 2** Lesson 8: Recognize Long *u* Vowel Teams Syllable Patterns (*u, ew, ue*)	16
Vowel Teams /o͝o/ (*oo, ou*)	115 (p. 116) 116 (p. 117)	**Grade 1** Lesson 27: Vowel Teams: /o͝o/ and /o͞o/	54
Variant Vowels /ŏ/ (*a, al, au, aw, augh*)	117 (p. 118) 118 (p. 119)	**Grade 1** Lesson 29: Identify and Name Vowel Sounds: *aw, au, al, augh*	58
		Grade 2 Lesson 21: Identify and Name Vowel Sounds: *aw, au, al, augh*	42
Contractions with *not*	119 (p. 120) 120 (p. 121)	See *Benchmark Advance* Print Concepts Intervention **Grade 2** Lesson 10: Distinguish Between Letters and Other Printed Symbols	20
Contractions with *'s, 're*	121 (p. 122) 122 (p. 123)	See *Benchmark Advance* Print Concepts Intervention **Grade 2:** Lesson 10: Distinguish Between Letters and Other Printed Symbols	20

Skill	Quick Check	***Benchmark Advance*** **PWR Intervention Lessons**	Page
Contractions with *'m, 'll, ve*	123 (p. 124) 124 (p. 125)	See *Benchmark Advance* Print Concepts Intervention **Grade 2** Lesson 10: Distinguish Between Letters and Other Printed Symbols	20
Compound Words	125 (p. 126) 126 (p. 127)	See *Benchmark Advance* Phonological Awareness Intervention **Grade 1** Lesson 12: Determine How Compound Words Are Formed	24
		See *Benchmark Advance* Phonological Awareness Intervention **Grade 2** Lesson 12: Determine How Compound Words Are Formed	24
Plural Nouns *-s, -es*	127 (p. 128) 128 (p. 129)	**Grade K** Lesson 49: Read Nouns with Inflectional Endings: *-s*	98
		Grade 1 Lesson 32: Read Nouns with Inflectional Endings: *-s* Lesson 35: Read Nouns with Inflectional Ending: *-es*	64 70
		Grade 2 Lesson 18: Decode Words with Inflectional Endings: *-es*	36
Irregular Plural Nouns	129 (p. 130) 130 (p. 131)	**Grade 2** Lesson 23: Identify and Decode Irregular Plural Nouns	46
Inflectional Endings (*-s, -ed, -ing*, no spelling change)	131 (p. 132) 132 (p. 133)	**Grade K** Lesson 49: Read Nouns with Inflectional Endings: *-s*	98
		Grade 1 Lesson 32: Read Nouns with Inflectional Endings: *-s* Lesson 33: Read Verbs with Inflectional Ending: *-s* Lesson 34: Read Verbs with Inflectional Endings: *-ed, -ing*	64 66 68
Inflectional Endings (*-ed, -ing*, dropping final *e*, double final consonant)	133 (p. 134) 134 (p. 135)	**Grade 2** Lesson 49: Identify and Name Inflectional Endings *-s, -ed, -ing*	98
Inflectional Endings (adding *-es*, changing *y* to *i*)	135 (p. 136) 136 (p. 137)	**Grade 2** Lesson 18: Decode Words with Inflectional Endings: *-ies*	36
Comparative Inflectional Endings *-er, -est*	137 (p. 138) 138 (p. 139	**Grade 2** Lesson 25: Identify and Name Inflectional Endings *-er, -est*	50
Possessives (singular and plural)	139 (p. 140) 140 (p. 141)	See *Benchmark Advance* Print Concepts Intervention **Grade 2** Lesson 10: Distinguish Between Letters and Other Printed Symbols	20

Grades K-2
Quick Check to Intervention Resource Map

Skill	Quick Check	*Benchmark Advance* PWR Intervention Lessons	Page
Closed Syllables	141 (p. 142) 142 (p. 143)	**Grade 1** Lesson 9: Identify and Name Closed Syllables	18
		Grade 2 Lesson 1: Identify and Name Closed Syllables	2
		Lesson 51: Identify and Name Closed Syllables	102
Vowel-C-e Syllables	143 (p. 144) 144 (p. 145)	**Grade 2** Lesson 15: Recognize Vowel-C-e Syllable Pattern	30
Open Syllables	145 (p. 146) 146 (p. 147)	**Grade 1** Lesson 21: Recognize Open Syllables	42
		Grade 2 Lesson 2: Recognize Open Syllables	4
		Lesson 64: Recognize Open Syllables	128
Vowel-*r* Syllables	147 (p. 148) 148 (p. 149)	**Grade 2** Lesson 13: Recognize *r*-controlled Syllable Patterns with Long *Ee*	26
		Lesson 14: Recognize *r*-controlled Syllable Patterns with Long *Aa*	28
Vowel Team Syllables	149 (p. 150) 150 (p. 151)	**Grade 2** Lesson 60: Recognize Long Vowel Teams and Single Letters with the Long *a* Sound	120
		Lesson 61: Recognize Long Vowel Teams and Single Letters with the Long *o* Sound	122
		Lesson 62: Recognize Long Vowel Teams and Single Letters with the Long *e* Sound	124
		Lesson 63: Recognize Long Vowel Teams and Single Letters with the Long *i* Sound	126
Consonant-*le* Syllables	151 (p. 152) 152 (p. 153)	**Grade 1** Lesson 31: Identify and Name Syllables with *le*	62
		Grade 2 Lesson 16: Identify and Name *LE* Syllables	32
		Lesson 75: Identify and Name Syllables with *le*	150
Prefixes: *un-*, *re-*, *dis-*	153 (p. 154) 154 (p. 155)	**Grade K** Lesson 51: Decode Words with Common Prefixes: *re-*	102
		Grade 1 Lesson 37: Decode Words with Common Prefixes: *re-*	74
		Grade 2 Lesson 28: Decode Words with Common Prefixes: *re-*	56

Skill	Quick Check	***Benchmark Advance* PWR Intervention Lessons**	Page
Endings *-er, -or*	155 (p. 156) 156 (p. 157)	**Grade 1** Lesson 38: Decode Words with Common Suffixes: *-er, -est*	76
		Grade 2 Lesson 25: Identify and Name Inflectional Endings *-er, -est*	50
		Lesson 50: Identify and Name Inflectional Endings *-er, -est*	100
		Lesson 71: Identify and Name Inflectional Endings *-er, -est*	142
Endings *-y, -ly*	157 (p. 158) 158 (p. 159)	**Grade K** Lesson 52: Decode Words with Common Suffixes: *-y*	104
		Grade 1 Lesson 39: Decode Words with Common Suffixes: *-ly*	78
		Grade 2 Lesson 26: Identify and Decode *-y* and *-ly* Suffixes	52
Suffixes: *-ful, -less*	159 (p. 160) 160 (p. 161)	**Grade K** Lesson 50: Decode Words with Common Suffixes: *ful, less*	100
		Grade 1 Lesson 40: Decode Words with Common Suffixes: *ful, less*	80
		Grade 2 Lesson 32: Decode Words with Common Suffixes: *ful, less*	64
High-Frequency Words	161–186 (pp. 162–187)	**Grades K–2** High-frequency word practice occurs in each mini-lesson. Students are asked to read and write/trace high-frequency words.	Ex.: 5, 45, 173

Name ______________________________ Date ____________________

1.	b	t	c	q	w	y
2.	a	s	f	r	j	g
3.	l	m	d	i	z	
4.	v	u	h	n	x	
5.	k	e	o	p		

____/26

Name ______________________ Date ______________

1.	L	E	G	P	T	K
2.	D	U	W	H	C	X
3.	M	Q	A	N	O	
4.	Y	F	Z	S	J	
5.	V	R	I	B		

____/26

Name ____________________ Date ____________

1.		h	v	m	k
2.		n	m	e	t
3.		m	c	s	g
4.	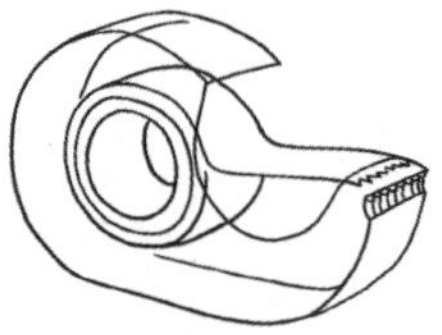	p	b	m	t
5.		d	w	y	m

___/5

Name ______________________________ Date ____________________

1.		mop	nap	bed
2.	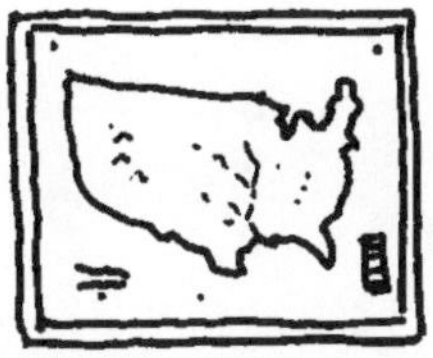	pen	can	mat
3.		but	him	mad
4.		mud	dam	nod
5.		ten	jot	hum

___/5

Quick Check #5

Name ______________________________ Date ____________________

1.	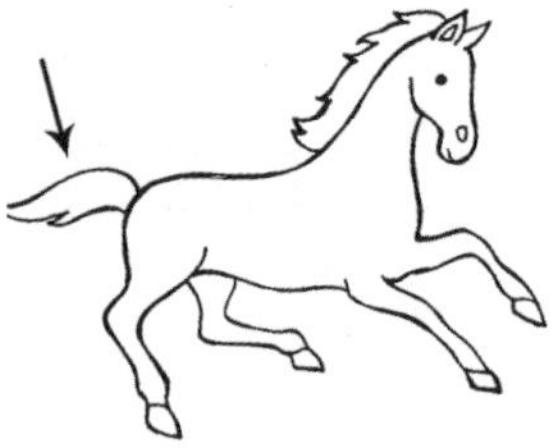	c	d	t	h
2.	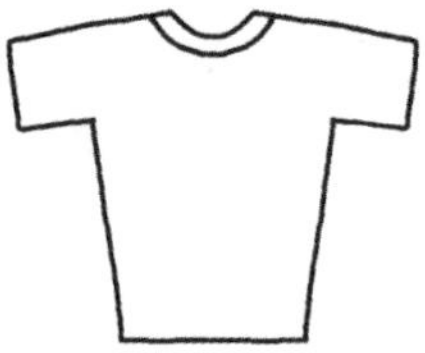	t	s	p	k
3.	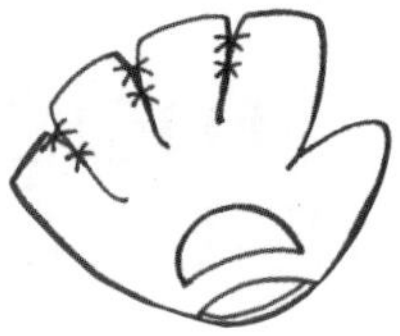	m	t	w	f
4.	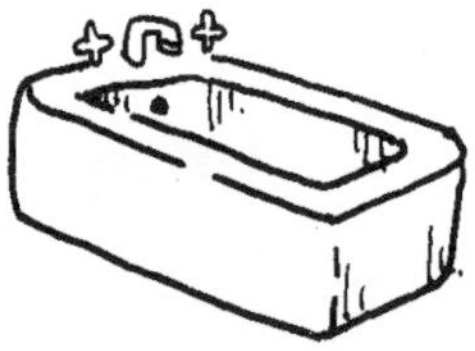	p	b	m	t
5.	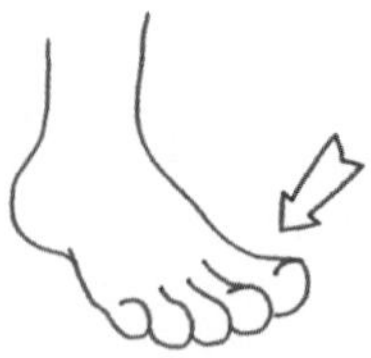	y	v	t	g

____/5

Name ______________________ Date ______________

1.	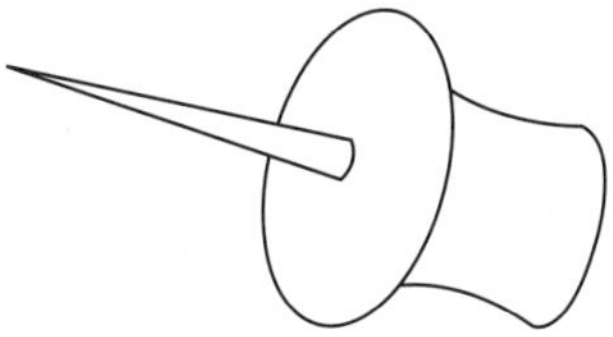	kid	tell	cat
2.	 2	pen	cat	tan
3.		tap	him	mad
4.	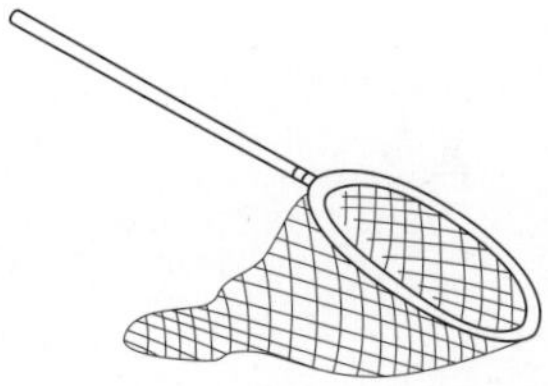	dam	nod	get
5.		wet	tap	pig

____/5

Name ______________________________ Date ____________________

1.		n	z	v	s
2.	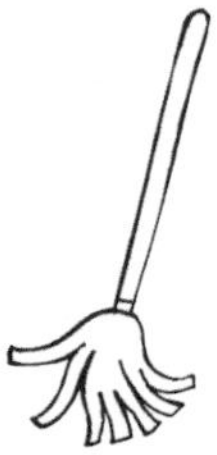	p	m	k	n
3.		m	l	n	t
4.		k	c	x	n
5.		s	n	t	w

____/5

Name ______________________ Date ______________

1.	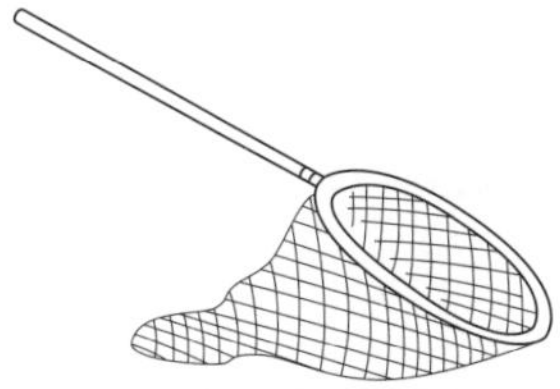	so	to	no
2.	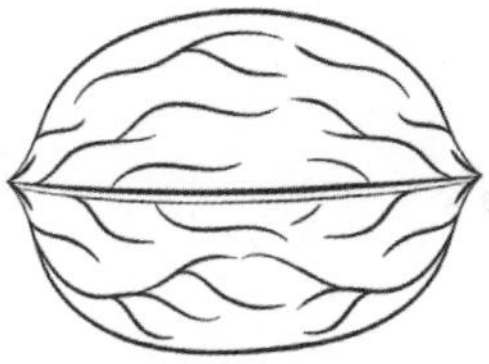	tub	nip	met
3.	 9	not	pen	rub
4.	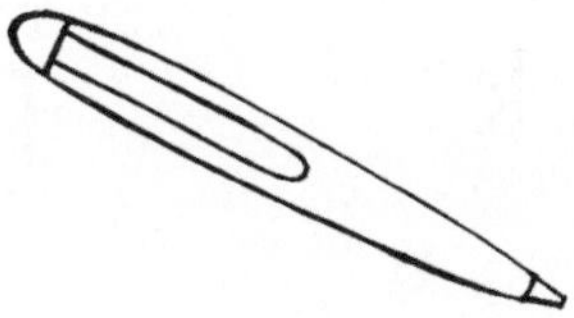	tin	big	set
5.		fog	nap	bun

___/5

Name ______________________________ Date ____________________

1.		g	p	d	q
2.	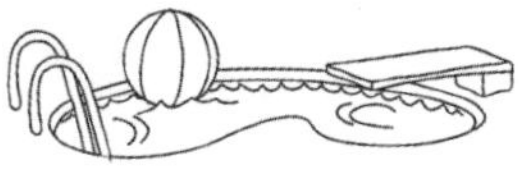	p	l	w	b
3.		m	s	p	t
4.		f	c	k	p
5.		z	p	s	b

____/5

Name ______________________________ Date ____________________

1.	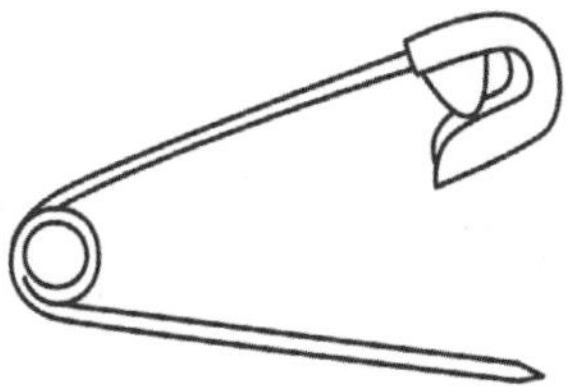	pad	not	cab
2.		run	cap	pet
3.		mad	pit	bun
4.	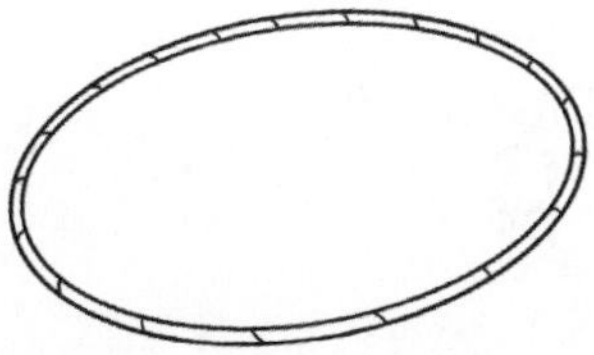	rip	sub	got
5.		kit	tap	web

____/5

Name ______________________________ Date ____________________

1.		h	b	l	s
2.		g	v	d	b
3.	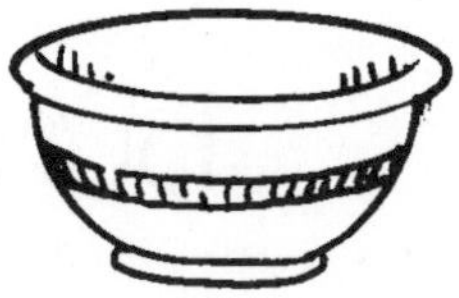	b	y	k	l
4.		h	b	p	t
5.		b	p	c	d

____/5

Name ______________________ Date ______________

1.	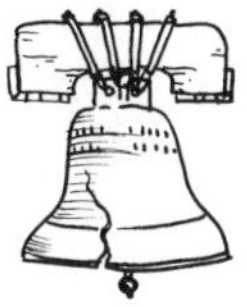	wet	lip	bud
2.		cop	ban	kit
3.	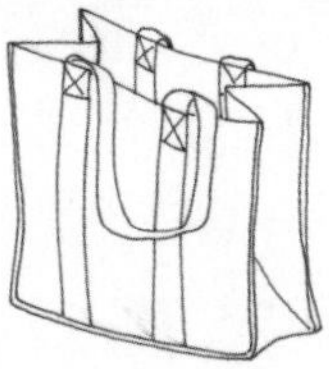	bit	gun	pat
4.		dab	not	him
5.		rap	dug	lob

____/5

Name ______________________________ Date ____________________

1.		g	p	d	k
2.	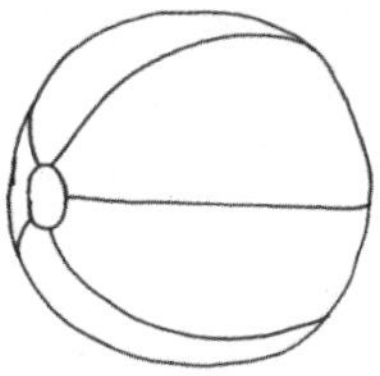	l	b	d	t
3.		d	r	w	n
4.		h	p	c	d
5.		s	d	k	f

____/5

Name ______________________________ Date ____________________

1.		dip	kid	log
2.		pod	fit	den
3.		mad	rim	dot
4.		nap	sun	wed
5.	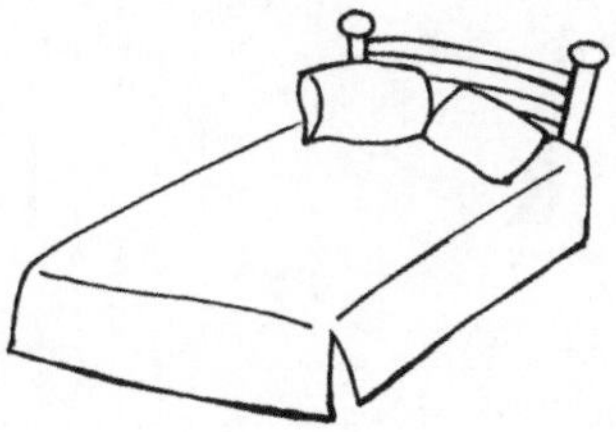	set	rod	big

___/5

Name ______________________ Date ______________

1.		k	t	g	j
2.		s	c	h	g
3.	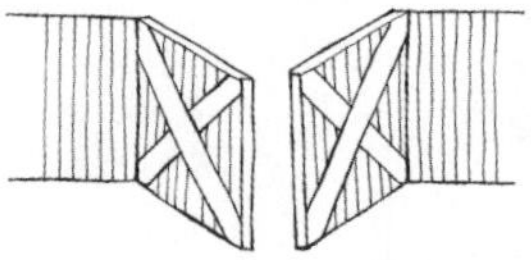	d	g	w	t
4.		g	p	n	d
5.		g	r	k	l

___/5

Name ________________________________ Date ____________________

1.		got	fun	hit
2.		men	dub	gap
3.		get	sit	win
4.	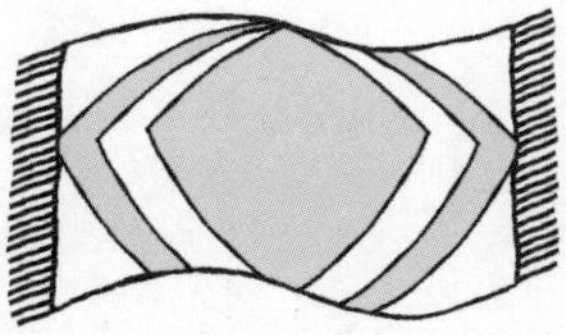	rat	fig	mob
5.		wag	rib	fun

____/5

Quick Check
#17

Name ______________________ Date ______________

1.		n	c	s	r
2.		t	s	l	v
3.		k	g	r	s
4.		p	s	q	f
5.	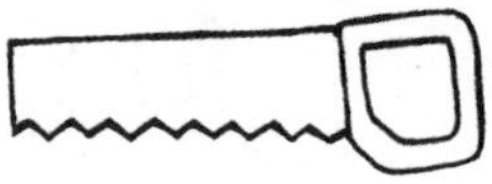	s	w	z	c

____/5

Name ______________________ Date ______________

1.	rip	tip	sip	lip
2.	cat	sat	bat	rat
3.	sum	hum	gum	mum
4.	lob	gob	sob	mob
5.	band	land	hand	sand

___/5

Name ______________________ Date ______________

1.		k	t	s	r
2.	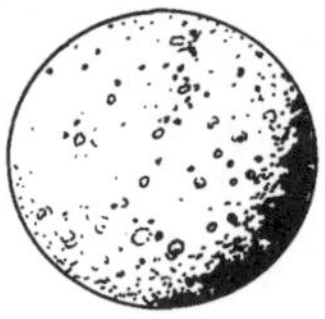	v	n	m	v
3.		g	x	r	w
4.		r	d	p	f
5.		s	z	r	c

____/5

Name ______________________________ Date ____________________

1.	pan	man	ran	tan
2.	rut	nut	gut	but
3.	lob	mob	sob	rob
4.	rim	dim	him	Tim
5.	sock	dock	rock	mock

___/5

Name ________________________________ Date ____________________

1.		p	h	t	f
2.		n	g	f	l
3.		f	s	h	d
4.		r	j	f	k
5.		c	n	w	r

____/5

Name ______________________ Date ______________

1.	pit	bit	fit	sit
2.	run	fun	bun	pun
3.	fog	dog	bog	nog
4.	bed	red	fed	Ted
5.	bake	fake	lake	cake

____/5

Name ______________________________ Date ____________________

1.		p	c	s	r
2.		v	b	h	c
3.		c	g	d	t
4.		l	x	y	f
5.		s	c	n	w

____/5

Name ______________________ Date ______________

1.	rap	tap	cap	lap
2.	cut	rut	nut	but
3.	rob	mob	cob	gob
4.	not	cot	got	rot
5.	same	came	name	tame

___/5

Name ______________________________ Date ____________________

1.		n	t	h	k
2.	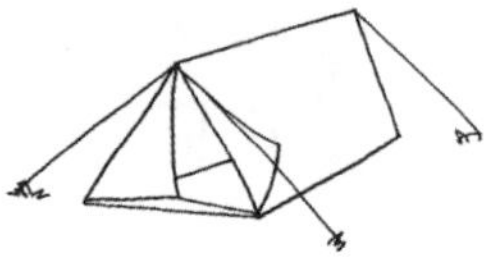	t	f	n	d
3.		h	l	r	m
4.		p	z	b	h
5.		s	b	h	j

____/5

Name ______________________ Date ______________

1.	not	hot	rot	got
2.	sip	rip	hip	tip
3.	had	bad	sad	fad
4.	rug	dug	bug	hug
5.	rim	him	dim	Tim

____/5

Quick Check
#27

Name ______________________ Date ______________________

1.		v	w	g	m
2.	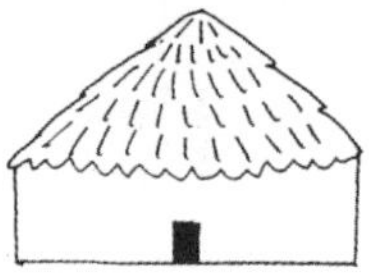	t	b	w	h
3.		w	u	p	x
4.		c	k	w	f
5.		s	d	l	w

___/5

Name ______________________ Date ______________

1.	win	fin	pin	bin
2.	seek	meek	peek	week
3.	tag	rag	wag	bag
4.	side	wide	ride	hide
5.	met	net	wet	get

___/5

Name ________________________ Date ____________________

1.		n	b	l	r
2.		t	l	g	k
3.		l	p	r	h
4.		f	b	h	r
5.	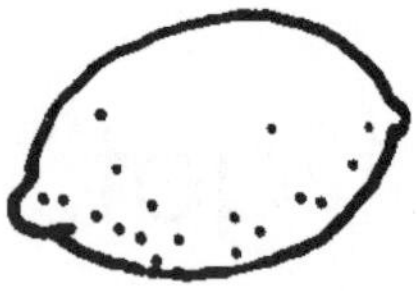	m	j	v	l

____/5

Name ______________________________ Date ____________________

1.	pet	let	wet	bet
2.	hog	dog	bog	log
3.	sick	pick	lick	nick
4.	lug	rug	bug	hug
5.	hand	land	sand	band

____/5

Quick Check
#31

Name ______________________________ Date ____________________

1.	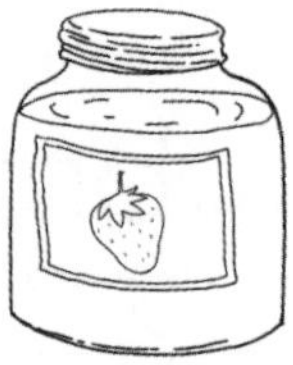	h	s	l	j
2.	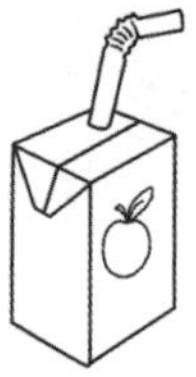	c	j	g	k
3.	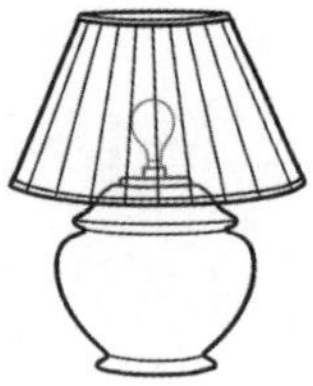	l	p	m	j
4.	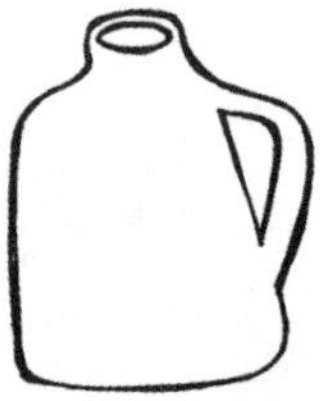	j	g	f	r
5.	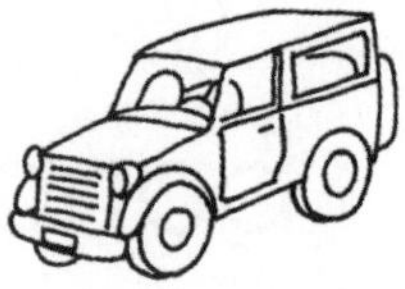	v	p	j	d

____/5

Name ______________________________ Date ____________________

1.	get	let	jet	bet
2.	jog	dog	hog	cog
3.	him	Tim	rim	Jim
4.	must	dust	just	rust
5.	cab	jab	lab	gab

____/5

Quick Check
#33

Name ______________________________ Date ____________________

1.		k	b	l	f
2.		n	b	g	k
3.		m	p	j	h
4.		f	r	h	k
5.		p	l	k	w

____/5

Name ______________________ Date ______________

1.	fit	lit	kit	wit
2.	miss	kiss	hiss	sis
3.	male	sale	kale	tale
4.	keen	seen	teen	been
5.	hid	bid	rid	kid

____/5

Name ______________________________ Date ____________________

1.		d	r	y	v
2.		w	y	l	k
3.	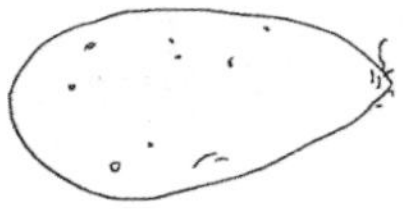	h	m	y	u
4.	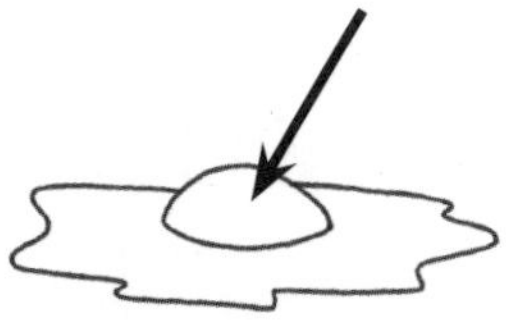	y	k	g	p
5.		r	j	y	z

____/5

Name ______________________________ Date ____________________

1.	met	yet	wet	jet
2.	rap	lap	nap	yap
3.	sell	fell	yell	well
4.	yip	rip	hip	lip
5.	hen	den	yen	Ken

____/5

Name ________________________________ Date ____________________

1.		w	n	v	r
2.		t	s	h	v
3.		v	w	b	c
4.		f	v	l	n
5.		p	t	j	v

____/5

Name ______________________________ Date ____________________

1.	hat	vet	sat	pat
2.	past	cast	vast	mast
3.	vane	mane	pane	cane
4.	rim	him	vim	dim
5.	note	vote	tote	dote

____/5

Quick Check
#39

Name ______________________________ Date ____________________

1.	teen	seen	green	queen
2.	wit	quit	fit	slit
3.	tail	snail	quail	hail
4.	quote	vote	note	tote
5.	trip	slip	quip	grip

___/5

Name ______________________________ Date ____________________

1.	bite	quite	mite	spite
2.	will	hill	grill	quill
3.	quack	track	stack	black
4.	wake	rake	take	quake
5.	vest	west	quest	nest

____/5

Name ______________________________ Date ____________________

1.		r	b	z	y
2.		x	z	p	q
3.	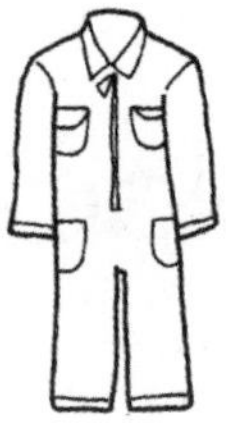	z	s	t	f
4.		u	c	v	z
5.		r	z	j	g

____/5

Name ______________________ Date ______________

1.	hip	yip	lip	zip
2.	bone	zone	lone	tone
3.	zap	rap	sap	cap
4.	room	broom	zoom	loom
5.	sack	hack	pack	Zack

____/5

Name ______________________ Date ______________

1.		y	b	z	x
2.		x	s	c	k
3.		b	k	x	f
4.		j	x	f	v
5.		s	z	d	x

____/5

Name ______________________ Date ______________

1.	fit	fig	fix	fin
2.	sap	sax	sat	sack
3.	mitt	Mick	miss	mix
4.	Rex	red	rest	ref
5.	fad	fall	fax	fast

___/5

Quick Check
#45

Name ________________________ Date ____________________

1.	hope	hole	hose	home
2.	sub	sum	sunk	suds
3.	rise	ride	ripe	rile
4.	said	says	sap	set
5.	him	hip	hit	his

____/5

Name ______________________ Date ______________

1.	wide	wife	wise	wipe
2.	peas	peat	peal	peak
3.	hat	had	has	ham
4.	rose	rope	robe	rode
5.	seed	seem	seen	sees

____/5

Name ________________________ Date ________________

1.	lot	loss	lock	lox
2.	duck	dump	dust	dub
3.	kit	kid	king	kick
4.	net	neck	nest	next
5.	pass	pad	pant	pack

____/5

Name ______________________ Date ______________

1.	pin	pick	pit	pig
2.	rock	rob	rot	rod
3.	lump	lug	luck	lull
4.	tap	tack	tan	tax
5.	den	desk	Deb	deck

___/5

Quick Check

#49

Name ______________________ Date ______________

1.	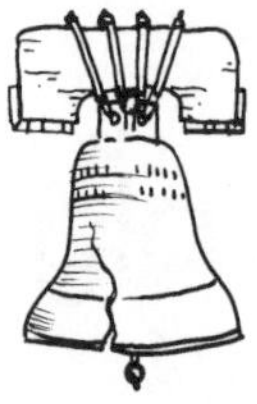	bb	ll	ss	tt
2.		xx	zz	tt	mm
3.		dd	ff	ck	lk
4.	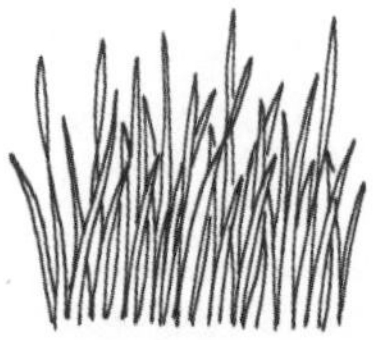	ss	zz	tt	ck
5.		hh	ll	zz	xx

____/5

Name ______________________________ Date ____________________

1.	mud	mutt	must	muck
2.	pass	pack	pad	pant
3.	cup	cut	cub	cuff
4.	tick	till	tip	tin
5.	led	left	less	legs

____/5

Name ______________________ Date ______________________

1.		fl	cl	sl	bl
2.		pl	gl	fl	sl
3.	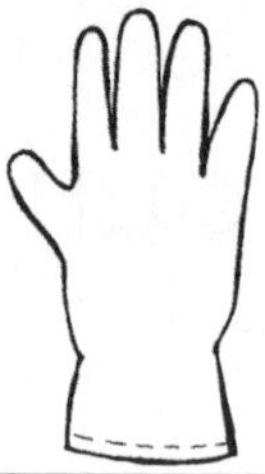	bl	gl	sl	pl
4.		cl	bl	gl	sl
5.		pl	fl	gl	bl

____/5

Name ______________________ Date ______________

1.	clip	flip	lip	slip
2.	plum	hum	glum	sum
3.	lad	mad	glad	fad
4.	cub	rub	club	tub
5.	flag	bag	lag	rag

___/5

Name ________________________________ Date ____________________

1.		sm	sp	sk	sn
2.		st	sp	sk	sm
3.		sw	sm	sn	sk
4.		sn	st	sp	sw
5.		sn	st	sp	sk

____/5

Name ______________________________ Date ____________________

1.	pot	spot	slot	got
2.	slug	bug	mug	snug
3.	sock	smock	block	dock
4.	skim	slim	swim	him
5.	spin	skin	win	fin

____/5

Name ______________________ Date ______________

1.		cl	tr	cr	gr
2.		cr	gr	gl	br
3.	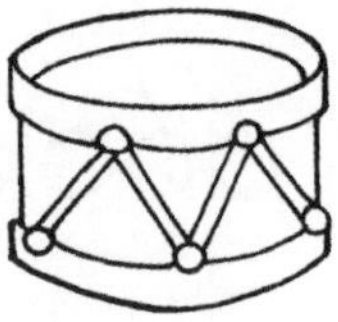	dr	br	pr	tr
4.		fr	pr	tr	cr
5.		gr	fr	br	dr

____/5

Name ______________________ Date ______________

1.	rap	flap	trap	tap
2.	trick	lick	stick	brick
3.	slim	grim	trim	rim
4.	stop	flop	drop	hop
5.	tree	free	flee	see

____/5

Name ______________________ Date ______________

1.		spl	spr	squ	str
2.		spr	spl	str	squ
3.	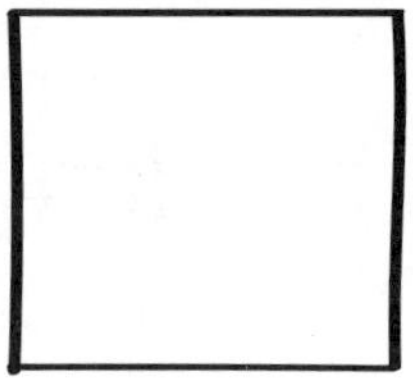	squ	str	spl	spr
4.		squ	spr	str	spl
5.	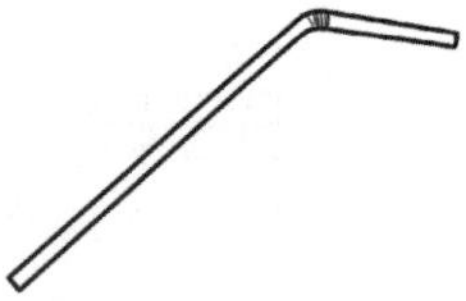	spl	squ	spr	str

____/5

Name ______________________ Date ______________

1.	slap	sap	strap	trap
2.	slit	spit	split	sit
3.	sting	spring	sing	string
4.	squid	slid	Sid	quit
5.	stay	spray	stray	say

____/5

Name ________________________ Date ________________

1.		sk	st	nt	sp
2.		nk	nt	nd	ld
3.		nd	nk	nt	sk
4.		sp	ll	nd	mp
5.		sk	st	mp	sp

____/5

Name ______________________ Date ______________

1.	west	went	when	wet
2.	just	jug	jump	junk
3.	lass	lap	lack	last
4.	desk	dent	deck	dens
5.	bat	band	back	bank

___/5

Name ______________________ Date ______________

1.		sl	sk	th	sh
2.		th	tr	sh	bl
3.		sh	ng	th	nk
4.	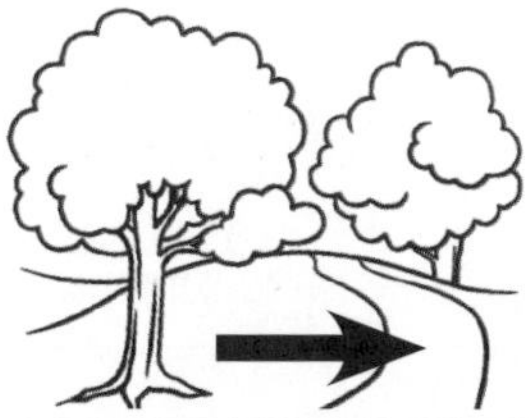	th	ng	sh	ck
5.		sk	th	st	sh

____/5

Name ________________________________ Date ____________________

1.	wish	wing	wink	wig
2.	bang	back	bash	bath
3.	cloth	clog	clock	clot
4.	log	long	lock	lost
5.	rust	rub	run	rush

____/5

Name ______________________________ Date ____________________

1.		sh	th	ch	wh
2.	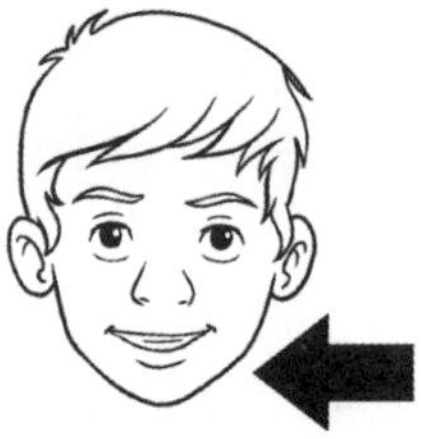	sh	ch	wh	th
3.		th	sh	ch	wh
4.		th	sh	tch	ck
5.		ch	th	ck	sh

____/5

Name ______________________________ Date ____________________

1.	must	muck	much	mutt
2.	pick	pink	ping	pitch
3.	bite	white	site	mite
4.	chill	hill	still	grill
5.	heel	feel	steel	wheel

____/5

Name ______________________ Date ______________

1.	**sip**	tent	cent	went
2.	**jet**	gem	hem	stem
3.	**page**	rich	ridge	risk
4.	**miss**	rage	rake	race
5.	**ledge**	wade	wage	wake

___/5

Name ______________________ Date ______________

1.	lake	late	lace	lane
2.	just	jump	jug	judge
3.	rice	ride	ripe	rite
4.	stake	stage	stamp	stack
5.	bash	back	bang	badge

____/5

Name ______________________________ Date ____________________

1.	**rap**	site	mite	write
2.	**nod**	kit	knit	mitt
3.	**neck**	gnat	get	what
4.	**dim**	lamp	lab	lamb
5.	**bun**	sick	sign	sink

____/5

Name ______________________ Date ______________

1.	trap	wrap	map	flap
2.	cot	slot	got	knot
3.	limp	limb	lip	lick
4.	dome	home	gnome	come
5.	climb	clip	click	cling

____/5

Quick Check
#69

Name ______________________ Date ______________

1.		sat	see	sew
2.		he	has	the
3.	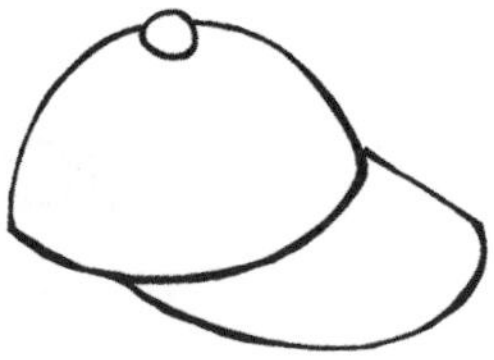	no	me	at
4.		is	have	go
5.	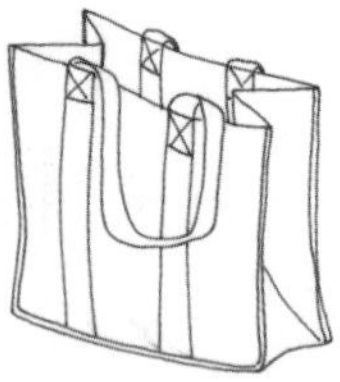	you	like	can

____/5

Name ______________________________ Date ____________________

1.	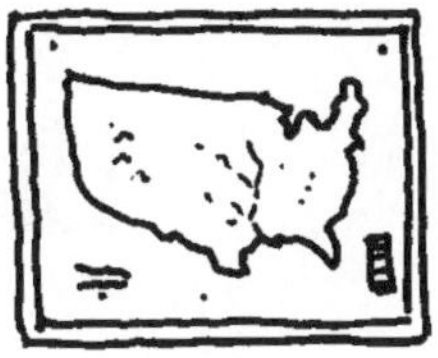	pat	pit	pot
2.		bed	bud	bad
3.	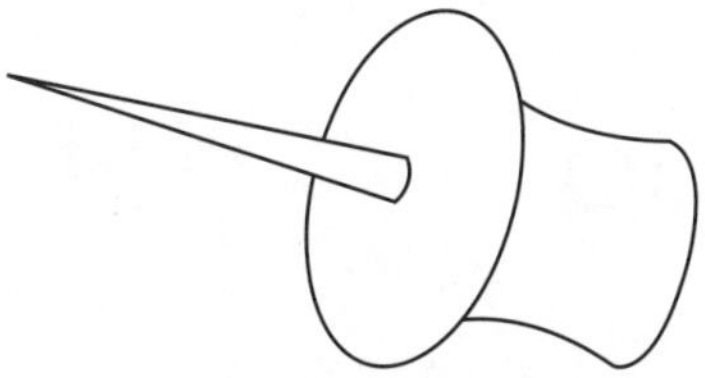	run	ran	Ron
4.		tan	ten	tin
5.		sip	soup	sap

____/5

Name ______________________ Date ______________

1.	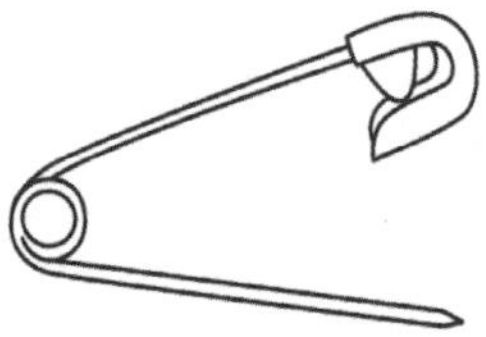	bag	be	big
2.		him	ham	he
3.	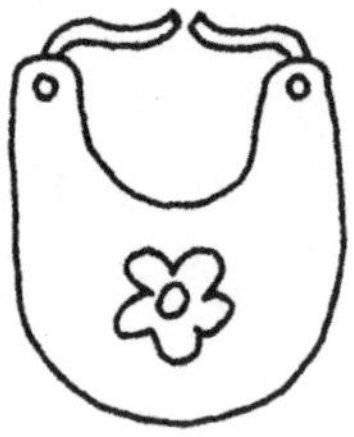	nap	nip	not
4.		hid	hat	hot
5.		sat	sit	see

___/5

Name ______________________ Date ______________

1.		fox	fix	fax
2.		dog	dug	dig
3.		bid	bad	bud
4.		pan	pen	pin
5.		jab	jib	job

____/5

Name ______________________ Date ______________

1.	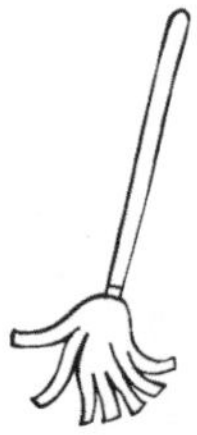	hot	hat	hit
2.		tip	tap	top
3.		sad	sod	said
4.		cot	cat	can
5.	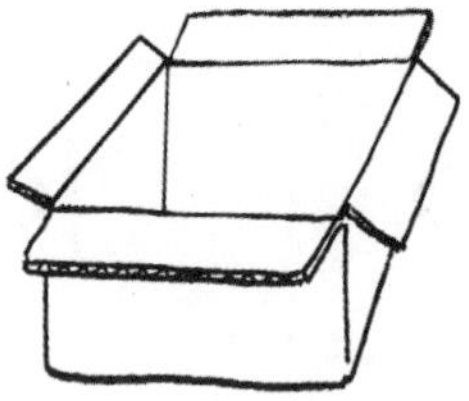	lit	like	lot

____/5

Name ______________________ Date ______________

1.	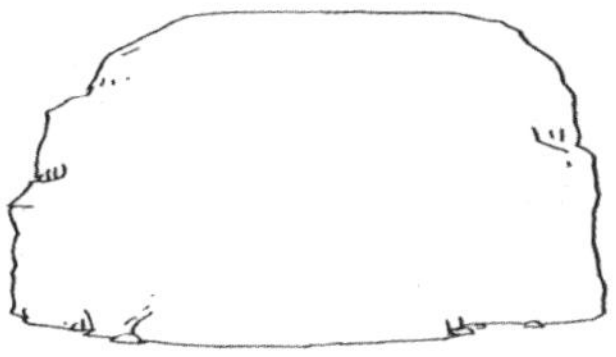	lag	look	lock
2.		red	rot	rut
3.		on	in	an
4.		net	nap	not
5.	•	cob	cab	can

____/5

Name ______________________________ Date ____________________

1.		sob	sub	said
2.		hut	hat	hot
3.		got	gut	go
4.		nut	not	Nat
5.		mad	my	mud

____/5

Name ____________________ Date ____________

1.	jog	jig	jug	jag
		cub	cob	cot
		lock	lack	luck
		run	Ron	win
5.	but	bat	bit	be

____/5

Name ______________________________ Date ____________________

1.	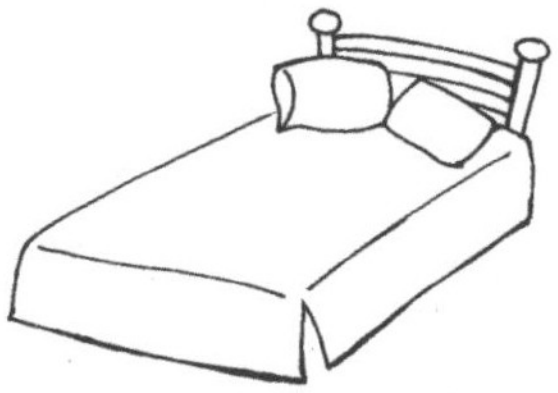	jet	jot	jut
2.	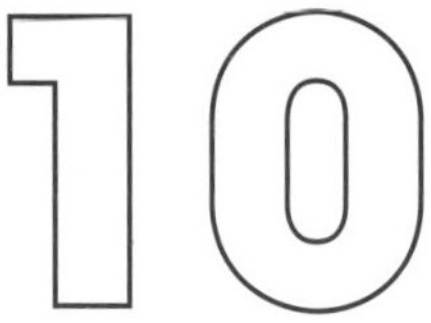 10	want	win	went
3.	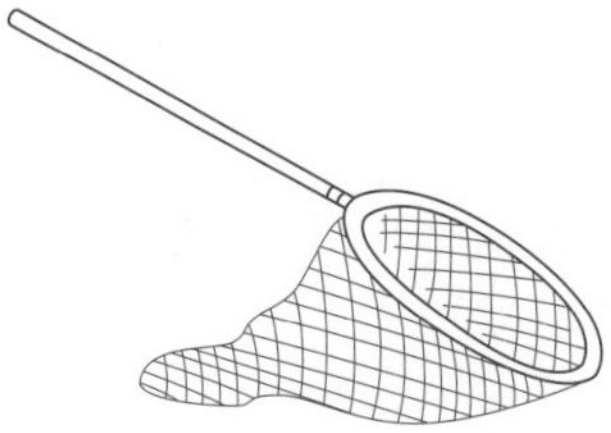	dock	duck	deck
4.	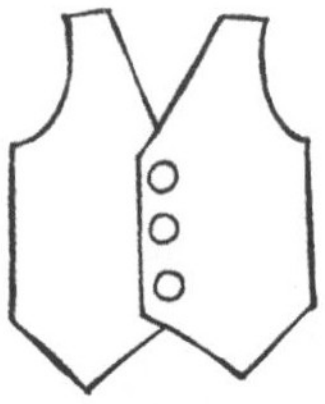	get	got	gut
5.	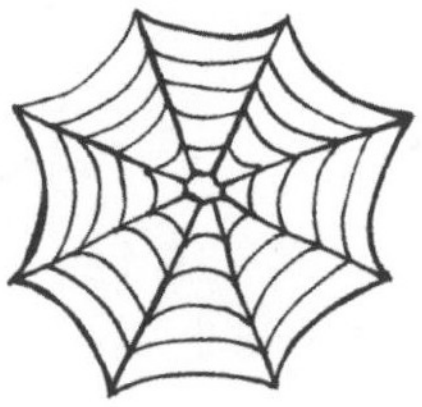	Sal	sill	sell

____/5

Name ______________________ Date ______________

1.	rid	rod	red	run
2.	den	did	Dan	Don
3.	bat	but	bit	bet
4.	will	well	want	we
5.	moon	my	men	mud

____/5

Quick Check
#79

Name ______________________________ Date ____________________

1.	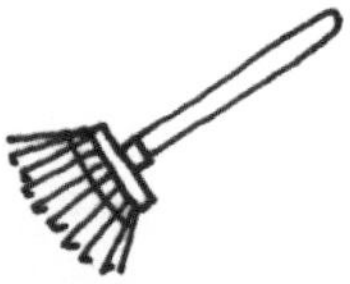	made	mud	mad
2.	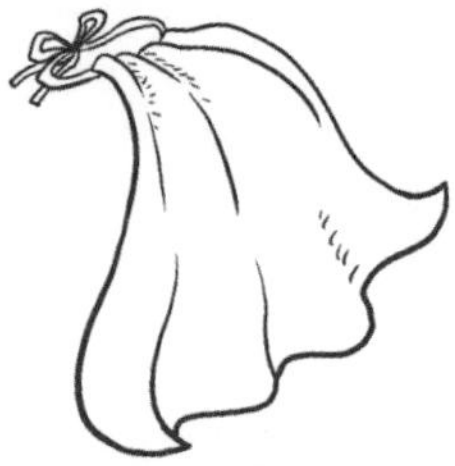	Tom	tame	Tim
3.	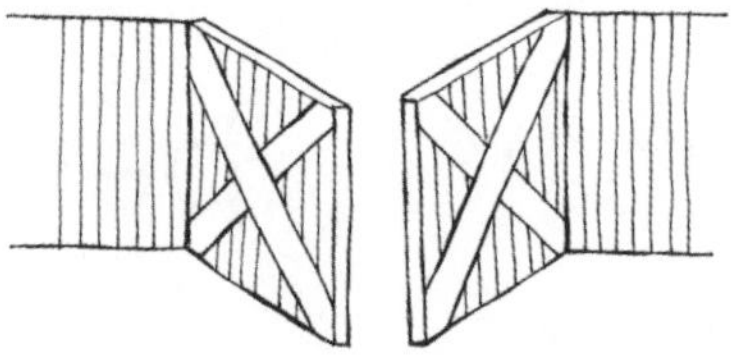	like	lake	lock
4.	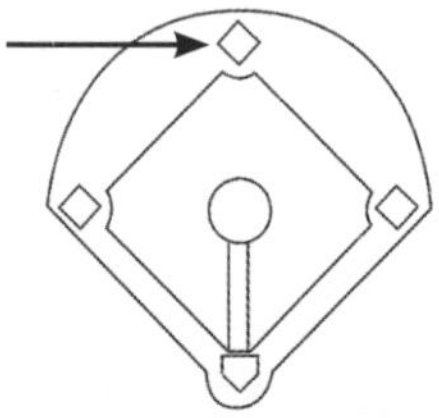	rot	rat	rate
5.	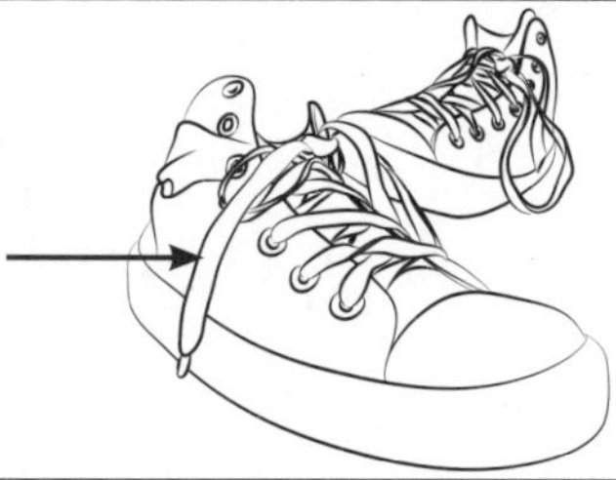	pane	pen	pun

____/5

Name ______________________________ Date ____________________

1.	let	lot	late	lit
2.	tap	top	tip	tape
3.	sell	sale	sill	sock
4.	cane	come	can	con
5.	back	buck	bake	big

____/5

Name ______________________________ Date ____________________

1.		male	mill	mole
2.		woke	wick	wake
3.	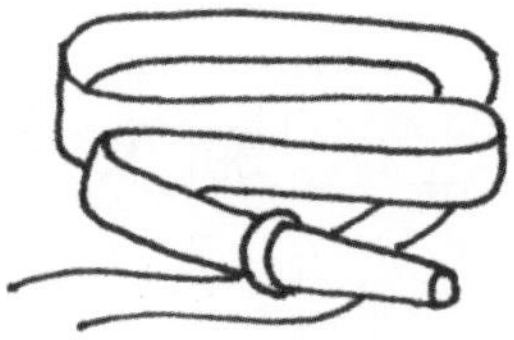	dim	dame	dome
4.		hope	hip	hop
5.	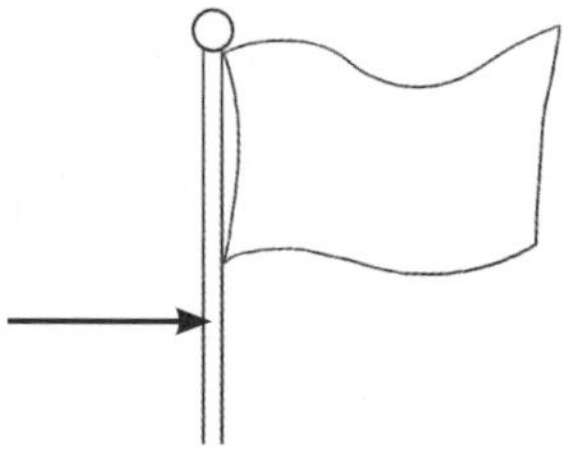	vat	vote	vet

___/5

Name ______________________ Date ______________

1.	can	con	cone	cane
2.	rub	robe	rib	rob
3.	hope	hip	hop	have
4.	Jake	joke	Jack	jot
5.	sell	sale	sill	sole

____/5

Quick Check

#83

Name ______________________ Date ______________

1.	 9	rap	rope	ripe
2.		mite	mate	mitt
3.		line	lane	lone
4.		tell	tile	tale
5.		wade	wed	wide

____/5

Name ______________________________ Date ____________________

1.	tame	Tim	time	Tom
2.	pile	pale	pole	pill
3.	lake	lock	look	like
4.	said	side	sad	sod
5.	mane	men	mine	man

____/5

Quick Check
#85

Name ______________________________ Date ____________________

1.	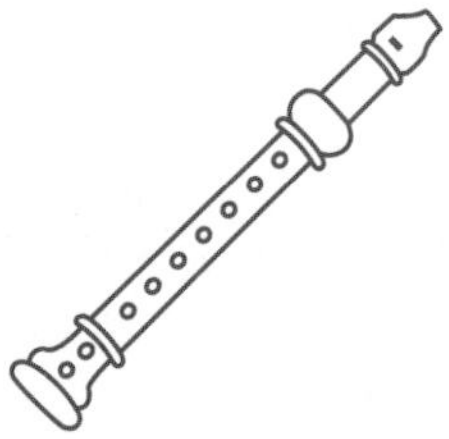	ride	rode	rude
2.	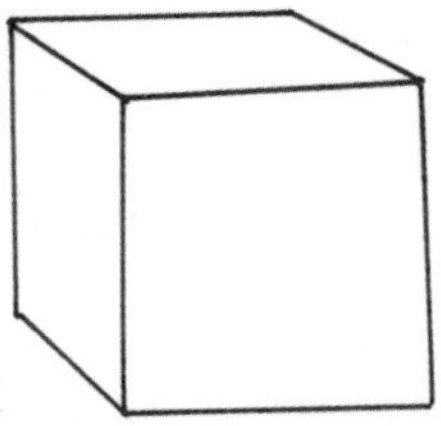	fuse	fuss	fun
3.	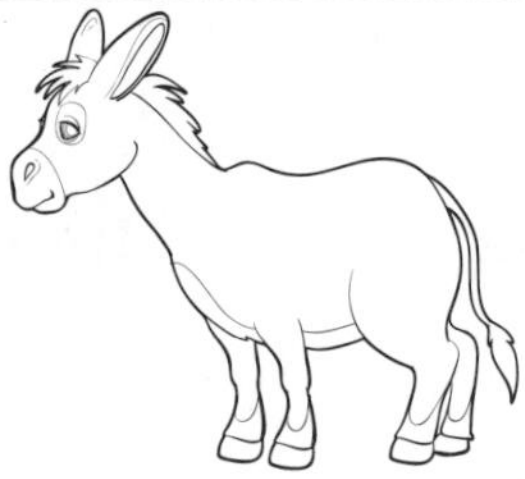	tune	tan	tone
4.	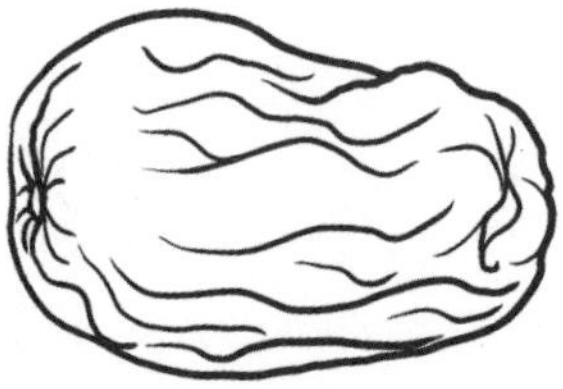	Dad	did	dude
5.	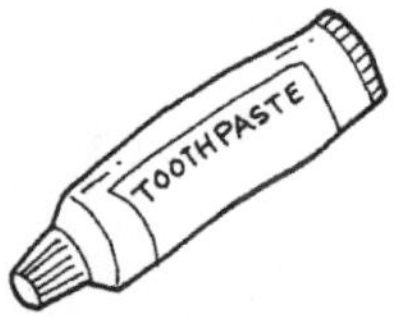	rule	rile	role

___/5

Name ______________________ Date ______________

1.	coat	cot	cute	cat
2.	fame	fan	fin	fume
3.	June	Jan	Jane	Jon
4.	tap	tube	tab	top
5.	mile	male	mute	mill

____/5

Quick Check
#87

Name ______________________ Date ______________

1.	**date**	sell	sail	sill	sole
2.	**name**	break	back	brick	broke
3.	**hail**	we	way	why	what
4.	**stay**	like	lick	lake	lock
5.	**great**	till	tell	tile	tail

____/5

Name ______________________ Date ______________

1.	ride	rode	red	raid
2.	me	may	my	mud
3.	tape	top	tip	tap
4.	wit	want	wait	what
5.	grit	great	got	get

____/5

Name ______________________ Date ______________

1.	**go**	tot	top	tow	to
2.	**soap**	cop	cap	crust	crow
3.	**low**	flat	flute	float	flit
4.	**toe**	rod	red	road	rude
5.	**coal**	no	net	nut	nay

____/5

Name ______________________ Date ______________

1.	lad	load	led	lid
2.	bell	bill	bale	bowl
3.	got	gets	goes	gas
4.	so	say	see	sun
5.	gray	grid	grow	grub

____/5

Name ______________________________ Date ____________________

1.	**see**	this	these	that	thus
2.	**tea**	wed	wide	we	wade
3.	**thief**	feel	fell	file	fail
4.	**he**	bed	bad	bead	bid
5.	**scene**	pack	piece	pick	peck

____/5

Name ______________________ Date ______________

1.	shut	shot	sheet	shade
2.	back	beak	bike	bake
3.	theme	Tom	them	Tim
4.	may	me	Moe	Ma
5.	filed	filled	failed	field

____/5

Name ______________________ Date ______________

1.	**money**	sea	say	so	sky
2.	**honey**	kept	kin	Ken	key
3.	**puppy**	we	way	why	when
4.	**valley**	leak	like	lake	lock
5.	**city**	fade	fly	feed	fit

____/5

Name ____________________ Date ____________

1.	fun	fine	funny	fan
2.	tuck	turkey	today	took
3.	jelly	jail	Jill	Joel
4.	ail	alley	away	all
5.	shine	shin	shiny	shoe

____/5

Name ______________________ Date ______________

1.	**pie**	may	me	my	Moe
2.	**time**	sit	sight	seat	set
3.	**fly**	lie	lee	law	low
4.	**ice**	fit	fate	fight	feet
5.	**high**	way	we	wit	why

____/5

Name ________________________________ Date ____________________

1.	by	be	bay	big
2.	mate	meet	might	mitt
3.	tea	tie	toe	tee
4.	hay	he	hoe	hi
5.	say	see	sigh	so

____/5

Quick Check
#97

Name ______________________________ Date ____________________

1.	**rule**	dull	die	due	dole
2.	**stew**	club	clay	clock	clue
3.	**tune**	knew	knit	know	knee
4.	**glue**	blow	blew	blog	bleed
5.	**huge**	few	fun	fit	feet

____/5

Name ______________________ Date ______________________

1.	say	so	sue	sun
2.	fly	flu	flow	flea
3.	true	try	tree	tray
4.	gray	grew	green	grow
5.	hay	how	hew	hoe

____/5

Name ______________________________ Date ____________________

1.		cat coat cart
2.		for far fan
3.		park pack poke
4.		ham harm him
5.		ban bone barn

___/5

Name ______________________________ Date ____________________

1.	had	hide	hard	her
2.	shape	ship	sheep	sharp
3.	part	pat	pet	peat
4.	tie	tar	tan	true
5.	make	Mack	mark	Mike

____/5

Name ______________________________ Date ____________________

1.		tar	tore	tire
2.	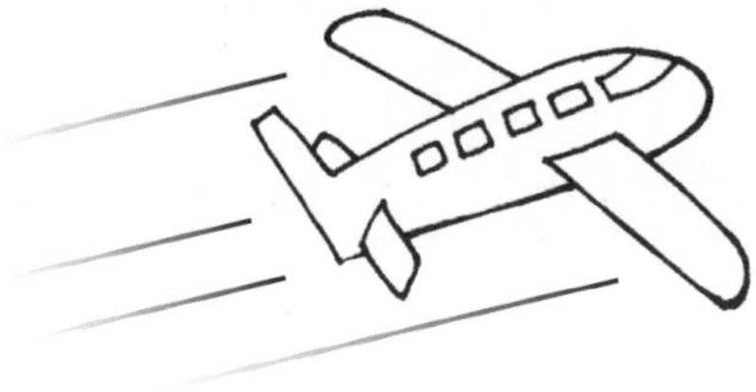	for	fire	far
3.	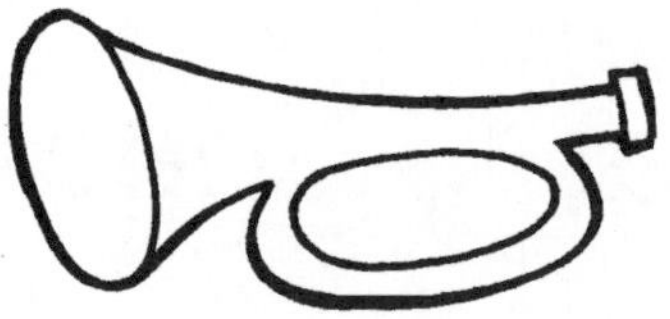	car	are	oar
4.	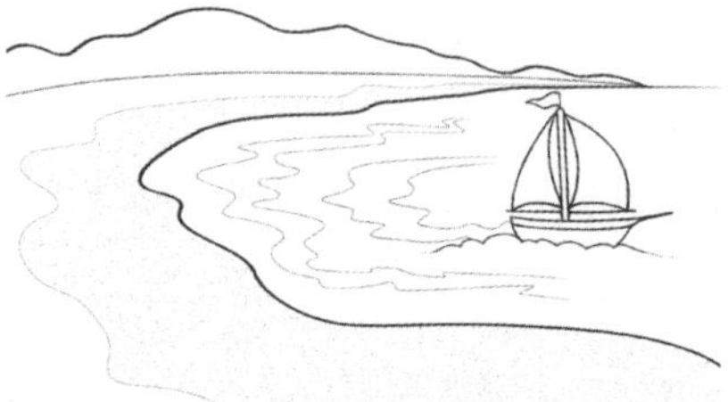	barn	bone	born
5.		core	car	cost

____/5

Name ______________________________ Date ____________________

1.	mar	more	mare	mark
2.	cord	code	card	car
3.	raw	red	row	roar
4.	tone	tar	torn	tire
5.	saw	score	sew	see

____/5

Quick Check
#103

Name ______________________________ Date ____________________

1.		curl	coal	call
2.	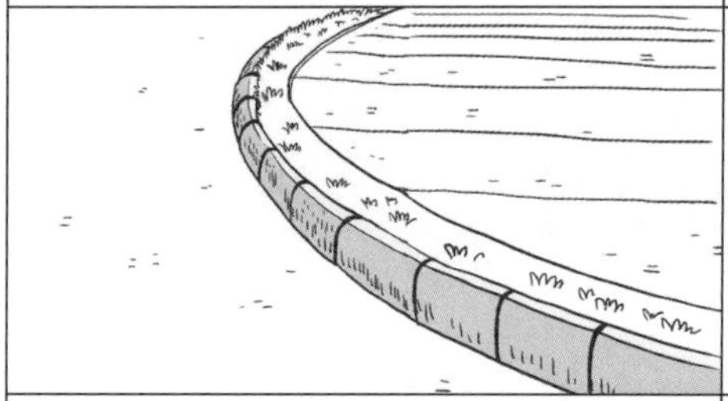	for	far	fur
3.		tore	turn	tar
4.		board	bird	bard
5.		hurt	hut	hart

____/5

Name ______________________________ Date ____________________

1.	nose	niece	nurse	nice
2.	wore	were	when	where
3.	shirt	short	sheet	shut
4.	bun	barn	burn	born
5.	dart	date	dirt	dot

____/5

Name ______________________________ Date ____________________

1.		nor	near	never
2.		peer	par	pore
3.		fore	fare	fear
4.	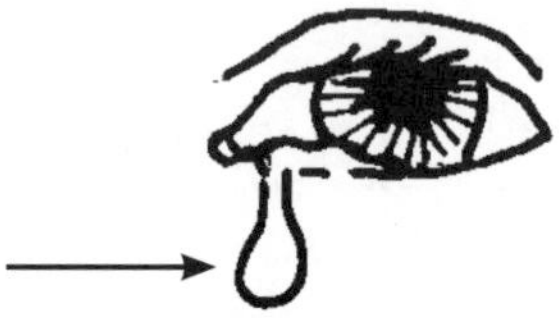	here	hire	hard
5.	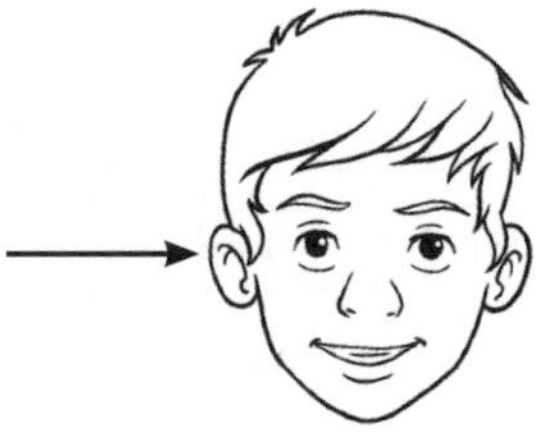	roar	rear	row

____/5

Name ______________________ Date ______________

1.	char	chore	churn	cheer
2.	gear	gore	girl	greed
3.	your	year	yap	yip
4.	smart	shore	smear	smirk
5.	more	mere	mare	mar

____/5

Name ______________________________ Date ____________________

	Picture	Words		
1.	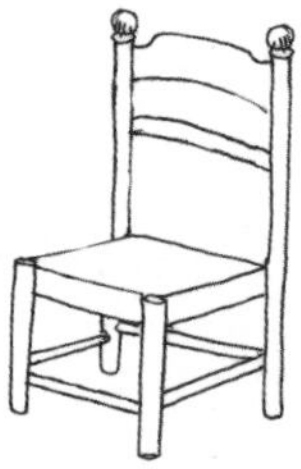	dear	dare	deer
2.	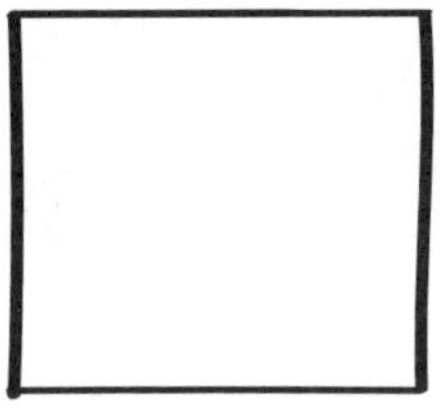	pair	par	pore
3.		car	care	core
4.		star	stir	stair
5.		wear	were	wire

____/5

Name ______________________ Date ______________

1.	shore	shear	share	sheer
2.	bore	burr	bar	bare
3.	there	then	those	that
4.	hire	hair	here	her
5.	mare	more	mar	mere

____/5

Name ______________________ Date ______________

1.		now	new	nay
2.		tone	tune	town
3.	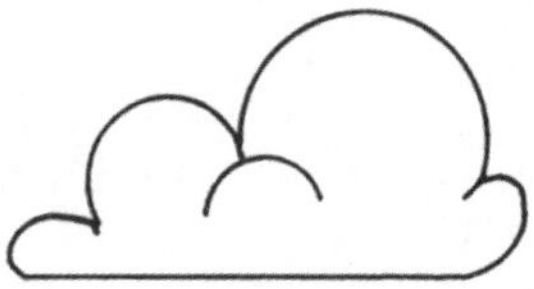	shot	shut	shout
4.		load	loud	lead
5.		bran	brown	brain

____/5

Name ____________________ Date ____________

1.	fond	find	fund	found
2.	dawn	down	done	dune
3.	grand	grind	ground	grin
4.	howl	hole	hall	hull
5.	put	pot	pat	pout

____/5

Name ______________________ Date ______________

1.		say	sue	soy
2.		point	paint	punt
3.		nose	noise	nice
4.		coal	call	coil
5.	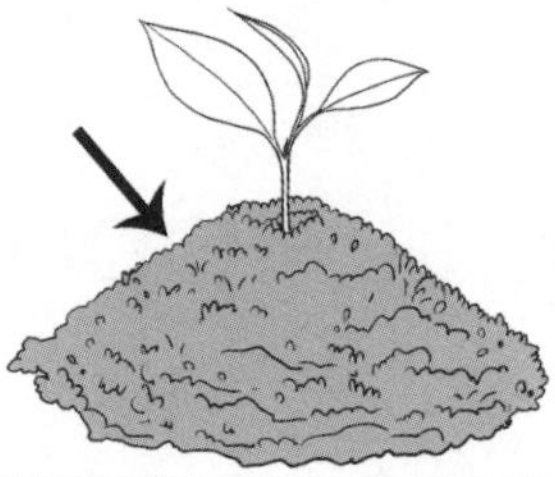	foil	foul	fall

____/5

Name ______________________________ Date ________________

1.	Joan	join	Jean	joke
2.	bowl	ball	bill	boil
3.	voice	vice	vase	visit
4.	Joe	jay	joy	Jon
5.	Ray	Roy	raw	row

___/5

Name ______________________________ Date ____________________

1.		sun	sign	soon
2.		food	fade	fad
3.		pool	pole	pail
4.		soap	sap	soup
5.	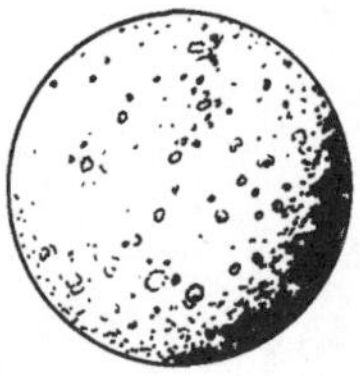	shoe	show	shy

____/5

Name ______________________ Date ______________

1.	lope	lap	leap	loop
2.	stole	stool	stall	stale
3.	group	grip	grape	gripe
4.	bad	broad	build	bed
5.	your	you	yawn	yarn

___/5

Name ______________________________ Date ____________________

1.		would	wade	wed
2.	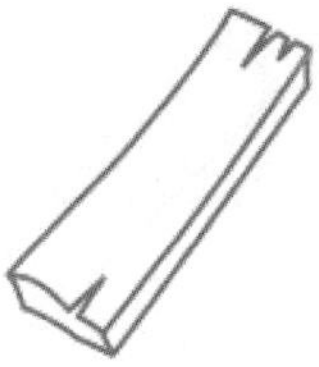	shake	shook	shock
3.	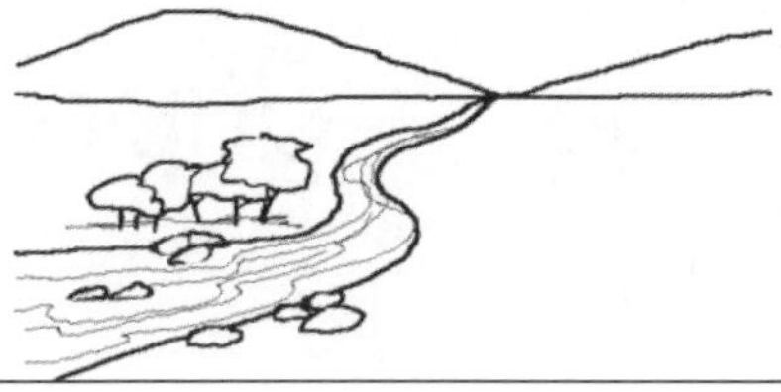	foot	fat	fate
4.		lock	luck	look
5.	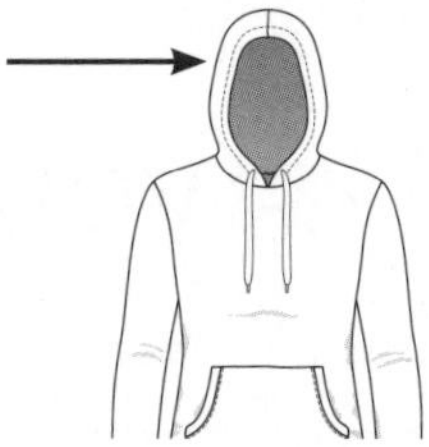	buck	book	bake

____/5

Name ______________________ Date ______________

1.	tuck	took	take	tack
2.	stand	stayed	stood	stud
3.	could	code	cud	cod
4.	well	wool	will	wall
5.	feet	fault	fate	foot

____/5

Name ______________________ Date ______________

1.		hail	haul	hole
2.		flaw	flow	flew
3.	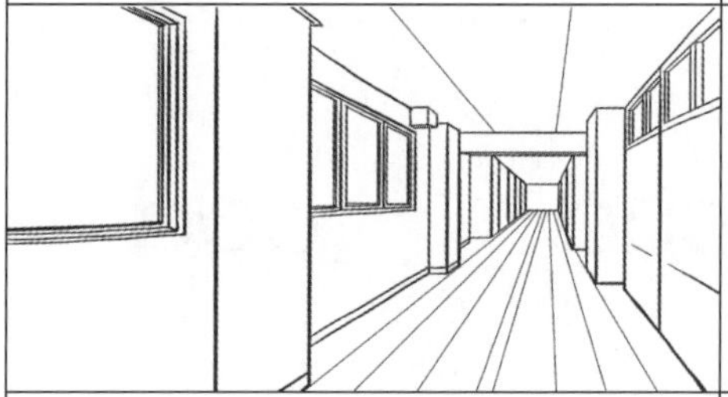	lawn	lone	loon
4.		ball	bell	bowl
5.		felt	fault	fool

____/5

Name ______________________________ Date ____________________

1.	tail	tall	tule	toll
2.	clay	clue	claw	clean
3.	coat	caught	cut	colt
4.	lunch	link	launch	long
5.	wake	walk	wick	woke

____/5

Name ______________________________ Date ____________________

1. Manny does not feel good. ______________

2. He can not go to the park. ______________

3. Kate has not called. ______________

4. Manny is not going to school. ______________

5. Mom will not let him go. ______________

____/5

Name ________________________________ Date ____________________

1. They _______ ready to leave for school.

weren't **can't** **won't**

2. Peter _______ find the book.

don't **isn't** **couldn't**

3. We ______ take our coats with us.

won't **aren't** **hasn't**

4. Mara _____ like her lunch.

wouldn't **doesn't** **weren't**

5. He _____ standing at the bus stop.

isn't **can't** **don't**

___/5

Name ______________________________ Date ____________________

1. You are going on a trip. ______________

2. He is happy to leave. ______________

3. Who is going to pack a bag? ______________

4. What are we planning to do? ______________

5. Here is a suitcase. ______________

___/5

Name ______________________________ Date ____________________

1. ________ going to school today.

   You's **You** **You're**

2. The teacher says _____ Friday.

   they're **she's** **it's**

3. I hope _____ enjoying the day.

   she **she's** **she're**

4. ______ done with our work.

   Weren't **We're** **We's**

5. _______ a turtle in our classroom.

   There's **What's** **Let's**

____/5

Quick Check
#123

Name ______________________________ Date ____________________

1. I will leave soon. ____________________

2. We have gone to the zoo. ____________________

3. They will go with us. ____________________

4. I am sure that is a snake. ____________________

5. You have got to see this! ____________________

____/5

Name ______________________ Date ______________

1. ________ going to the lake with Jen.

I'll **I've** **I'm**

2. ________ bring a blanket.

She's **She** **She'll**

3. ________ give me a ride.

They'll **They're** **They've**

4. ________ packed a lunch.

I'll **I've** **I'm**

5. ________ got toys and games to play.

We're **We'll** **We've**

____/5

Quick Check
#125

Name ______________________________ Date ____________________

1. The <u>bookcase</u> in our room is full. ______________

2. We went to the <u>airport</u> in the morning. ______________

3. My mother asked me to sing <u>something</u>. ______________

4. These cookies are <u>homemade</u>. ______________

5. I am going to the park <u>without</u> my dog. ______________

___/5

Name ______________________________ Date ____________________

1. I did not see my coat any_______.

one **where** **how**

2. _______times I lose my hat.

Some **Mean** **Any**

3. Mom wants us to put _______thing away.

every **little** **one**

4. Can any_______ help me find it?

way **one** **place**

5. I am going to the park this after_______.

time **noon** **school**

___/5

Name ______________________ Date ________________

1. We saw two ______________ in the field.

fox **foxs** **foxes**

2. Those ______________ are my friends.

boy **boys** **boyes**

3. Mom asked me to wash all of the ______________.

dish **dishs** **dishes**

4. We got a new table and four ______________.

chair **chairs** **chaires**

5. Dad ate two ______________ for lunch.

peach **peachs** **peaches**

____/5

Name ______________________ Date ______________

1. Nina made three ______________.
wish

2. The ______________ are next to the wall.
bench

3. We opened all of the ______________.
box

4. I put the ______________ into a bag.
chip

5. Two ______________ flew around the light.
moth

___/5

Name ______________________________ Date ____________________

1. Two ______________ swam across the pond.

goose **gooses** **geese**

2. Our cat catches lots of ______________.

mouse **mice** **mouses**

3. I brush my ______________ before I go to bed.

tooth **tooths** **teeth**

4. Five ______________ came out of the barn.

sheep **sheeps** **sheepes**

5. There are 22 ______________ in our class.

childs **childes** **children**

___/5

Name ______________________ Date ______________

1. Those ______________ got on the bus.
   man

2. The new books are on the ______________.
   shelf

3. He put socks on both ______________.
   foot

4. We jumped into the pile of ______________.
   leaf

5. We saw three ______________ cross the road.
   wolf

____/5

Name ______________________________ Date ____________________

1. Fiona ______________ pizza for lunch.

wants **wantes** **wanting**

2. Cindy ______________ over the wall.

jumped **jumpped** **jumping**

3. Kevin ______________ his room every day.

clean **cleans** **cleanes**

4. Leon's little boat ______________ across the pond.

sail **sailled** **sailed**

5. Pilar is ______________ out the window.

peek **peeks** **peeking**

____/5

Name ______________________ Date ______________

1. He always ______________ the right answers.
know

2. The ball is ______________ in the water.
float

3. How many people are ______________?
speak

4. Kim ______________ when she sees me.
shout

5. Yesterday, Tommy ______________ home.
walk

___/5

Name ______________________ Date ______________

1. Alma ______________ all the way to school.

skip **skiped** **skipped**

2. Danny is ______________ on the bus.

riding **rideing** **ridding**

3. We ______________ at the corner.

stoped **stopped** **stoping**

4. Two kids were ______________ to the bus driver.

waving **waveing** **wavving**

5. A man was ______________ on the sidewalk.

joging **jogging** **jogeing**

____/5

Name ______________________________ Date ____________________

1. Lynn is ________________ at you.
smile

2. The boys ________________ after the show.
clap

3. Children were ________________ in their seats.
sit

4. Mr. Burns ________________ to come, but I did not see him.
plan

5. I am ______________ a thank-you note.
write

____/5

Name ______________________________ Date ____________________

1. The baby ______________ every night.

crys **cryes** **cries**

2. Tell me some ______________.

storys **stories** **storyes**

3. We have two ______________ in our town.

librarys **libraryes** **libraries**

4. Mrs. Curry has five ______________ to give away.

puppies **puppys** **puppyes**

5. That movie was about two ______________.

spys **spyes** **spies**

____/5

Name ______________________________ Date ____________________

1. We went to pick ________________.
berry

2. Two ________________ helped us.
lady

3. I have three ________________.
penny

4. Ken saw two ________________.
pony

5. Meg picked some ________________.
daisy

____/5

Name ______________________________ Date ____________________

1. I chose the ______________ tent of all.

   small **smaller** **smallest**

2. You are ______________ than I am.

   tall **taller** **tallest**

3. Roses are the ___________ flowers in the whole garden.

   pretty **prettier** **prettiest**

4. That is the ______________ tree in the world!

   big **bigger** **biggest**

5. This blanket is ______________ than that one.

   soft **softer** **softest**

____/5

Name ______________________________ Date ____________________

1. I am the ______________ runner on the team.
fast

2. My pencil is ________________ than yours.
sharp

3. This is the _______________ coin in the whole bag.
shiny

4. Her backpack is ______________ than his.
light

5. Duke is the ______________ dog I know.
happy

____/5

Name ______________________________ Date ____________________

1. The ______________ coat was on the bench.

girls **girl's** **girls'**

2. The ______________ park was busy.

childrens **children's** **childrens'**

3. All of the ______________ seats were broken.

swings **swings's** **swings'**

4. We used the ______________ leash at the park.

dogs **dog's** **dogs'**

5. My ______________ car was parked nearby.

familys **family's** **familys'**

____/5

Name ______________________________ Date ____________________

1. The ______________ horns were loud.
   car

2. I rode my ______________ bike.
   sister

3. All of my ______________ bikes are red.
   friends

4. The ______________ scooter was fast.
   boy

5. He put gas into the ______________ tank.
   truck

____/5

Name ______________________ Date ______________

1.	napkin	dentist
2.	sunset	pumpkin
3.	pencil	contest
4.	rubber	until
5.	cobweb	bedbug

____/10

Name ______________________________ Date ____________________

1.	button	cannot
2.	insect	cactus
3.	sudden	himself
4.	pennies	happen
5.	subway	kitten

____/10

Name ______________________ Date ______________

1.	admire	sunrise
2.	explode	costume
3.	inside	tadpole
4.	excuse	nickname
5.	conclude	pancake

___/10

Name ______________________ Date ______________________

1.	mistake	suppose
2.	beware	bedtime
3.	homemade	include
4.	decide	compare
5.	mistake	someplace

____/10

Name ______________________________ Date ____________________

1.	baby	open
2.	spider	table
3.	paper	moment
4.	silent	pony
5.	music	remind

____/10

Name ______________________________ Date ____________________

1.	solo	wavy
2.	rotate	remove
3.	label	item
4.	human	motor
5.	notice	zero

____/10

Name ______________________ Date ______________

1.	perform	urgent
2.	forest	turnip
3.	stairway	berry
4.	thunder	nursing
5.	fairness	artist

___/10

Name ______________________________ Date ____________________

1.	order	birthday
2.	marble	thirsty
3.	surfer	forty
4.	purple	turkey
5.	explore	perfect

____/10

Quick Check
#149

Name ______________________________ Date ____________________

1.	detail	rowboat
2.	money	teacher
3.	playmate	foamy
4.	easy	between
5.	lookout	untie

____/10

Name ______________________________ Date ____________________

1.	valley	delight
2.	hockey	mailbox
3.	eighty	below
4.	relieve	people
5.	roadway	haystack

____/10

Name ________________________ Date ____________________

1.	paddle	buckle
2.	apple	settle
3.	juggle	circle
4.	rumble	sparkle
5.	tangle	cable

____/10

Name ______________________ Date ______________

1.	eagle	pickle
2.	huddle	little
3.	table	ankle
4.	single	tumble
5.	bottle	bugle

___/10

Name ______________________________ Date ____________________

un-	re-	dis-

1. May I ____fill my water bottle?

2. I like carrots, but I ____like cabbage.

3. You did not finish the game. That is ____fair!

4. Nick ____agrees with the answer to the question.

5. Duke is the ____friendly dog I know.

6. Rosa wants to ____write her letter.

____/6

Name ______________________________ Date ____________________

1. Gina was ____able to ride her bike.

un- **re-** **dis-**

2. That dog was here, but then it ____appeared.

un- **re-** **dis-**

3. Marco plans to ____paint the wall green.

un- **re-** **dis-**

4. Sometimes my brother ___obeys the rules.

un- **re-** **dis-**

5. Paula wants to ___visit the museum next week.

un- **re-** **dis-**

6. Ms. Field is ____happy with her sister.

un- **re-** **dis-**

___/6

Quick Check
#155

Name ______________________________ Date ____________________

-er	-or

1. Diane is a good baseball play____.

2. Our school had a visit____ yesterday.

3. Mr. Miller is the direct____ of the movie.

4. Grandpa says I am a hard work____.

5. Pete's dad is a build____.

6. Merrill wants to be an act____ on TV.

____/6

Name ______________________ Date ______________

1. That man is a great paint____.

-er **-or**

2. My uncle is a tail____.

-er **-or**

3. Mrs. Bland is my favorite teach____.

-er **-or**

4. They sold the house, but who was the buy____?

-er **-or**

5. My brother wants to be a sail____.

-er **-or**

6. Mr. Lopez is an edit____ for a newspaper.

-er **-or**

____/6

Quick Check
#157

Name ______________________________ Date ____________________

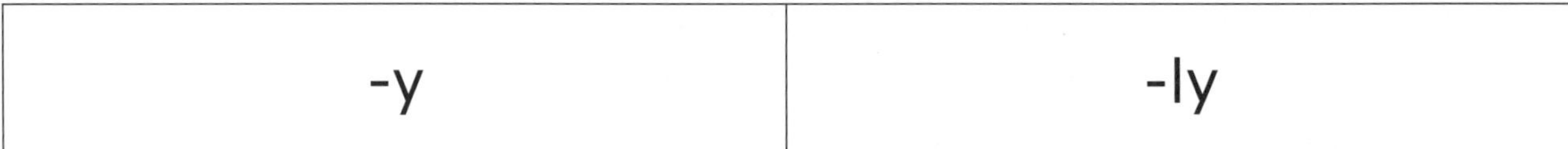

-y	-ly

1. It was very snow____ last winter.

2. The coach yelled loud____.

3. Hugo ran as quick____ as he could.

4. That drink tastes fruit____.

5. Gail did not speak very clear____.

6. This game is kind of trick____.

____/6

Name ______________________________ Date ____________________

1. This road is really bump____.

   -y **-ly**

2. Dad had to drive slow____.

   -y **-ly**

3. Mom told us to dress warm____.

   -y **-ly**

4. My little sister was being sneak____.

   -y **-ly**

5. Nick treats everyone fair____.

   -y **-ly**

6. This old bike is getting rust____.

   -y **-ly**

____/6

Name ______________________________ Date ____________________

-ful	-less

1. Glen was so thank____ for his gifts.

2. I am hope____ we can win the game.

3. The storm last night was power____.

4. Max is brave and fear____!

5. We had a wonder____ day at the zoo.

6. That dog looks scary, but he is harm____.

____/6

Name ______________________________ Date ____________________

1. Dad felt help____ when the tornado hit.

   -ful **-less**

2. A flashlight is use____ when the power goes out.

   -ful **-less**

3. Fran left the door open. That was care____.

   -ful **-less**

4. We were joy____ when the storm ended.

   -ful **-less**

5. That old radio is worth____.

   -ful **-less**

6. Marissa is so grace____ when she dances.

   -ful **-less**

____/6

Name ______________________ Date ______________

1.	we	like	the
2.	see	I	go

____/6

Name ______________________ Date ______________

1.	the	we	see
2.	go	she	can
3.	is	a	he
4.	has	play	little

____/12

Name ______________________________ Date ____________________

1.	he	has	play
2.	little	and	you
3.	with	big	for
4.	no	jump	one

____/12

Name ______________________________ Date ____________________

1.	for	no	jump
2.	one	have	are
3.	said	two	look
4.	me	come	here

____/12

Name ______________________________ Date ____________________

1.	look	me	come
2.	here	to	my
3.	of	what	put
4.	want	this	saw

____/12

Name ________________________________ Date ____________________

1.	I	like	the
2.	we	see	go
3.	she	can	is
4.	a	he	has
5.	play	little	and
6.	you	with	big
7.	for	no	jump
8.	one	have	are
9.	said	two	look
10.	me	come	here
11.	to	my	of
12.	what	put	want
13.	this	saw	

____/38

Name ______________________ Date ______________________

1.	the	see	go
2.	she	and	play
3.	little	you	with
4.	for	no	jump
5.	one	have	

___/14

Name ______________________________ Date ____________________

1.	are	said	two
2.	look	me	come
3.	here	to	my
4.	of	what	put
5.	want	this	saw

____/15

Name ______________________ Date ______________

1.	now	do	which
2.	went	was	there
3.	then	out	who
4.	good	by	them

____/12

Name ______________________________ Date ____________________

1.	were	our	could
2.	these	once	upon
3.	hurt	that	because
4.	from	their	when

____/12

Quick Check
#171

Name ______________________________ Date ____________________

1.	why	many	right
2.	start	find	how
3.	over	under	try
4.	give	far	too

____/12

Name ______________________________ Date ____________________

1.	after	call	large
2.	her	house	long
3.	off	small	brown
4.	work	year	live

____/12

Name ______________________________ Date ____________________

1.	found	your	know
2.	always	all	people
3.	where	draw	again
4.	round	they	country

____/12

Quick Check
#174

Name ______________________ Date ______________

1.	four	great	boy
2.	city	laugh	move
3.	change	away	every
4.	near	school	earth

___/12

Name ________________________ Date ________________

1.	before	done	about
2.	even	walk	buy
3.	only	through	does
4.	another	wash	some

___/12

Name ______________________________ Date ____________________

1.	better	carry	learn
2.	very	mother	father
3.	never	below	blue
4.	answer	eight	any

____/12

Name ______________________________ Date ____________________

1.	a	can	and
2.	come	are	for
3.	big	go	has
4.	I	have	is
5.	jump	my	one
6.	put	the	want
7.	what	you	he
8.	like	little	no
9.	of	saw	this
10.	to	we	with

____/30

Name ______________________________ Date ____________________

1.	here	look	me
2.	play	said	see
3.	she	try	about
4.	because	after	before
5.	call	do	earth
6.	father	give	her
7.	know	large	many
8.	near	off	people
9.	right	school	that
10.	two	under	very

____/30

Quick Check
#179

Name ______________________ Date ______________

1.	again	below	carry
2.	does	eight	find
3.	good	house	laugh
4.	mother	move	never
5.	once	round	small
6.	their	too	walk
7.	where	year	all
8.	away	better	by
9.	change	done	even
10.	found	learn	only

____/30

Name ______________________ Date ______________

1.	long	now	our
2.	some	them	through
3.	upon	was	when
4.	work	always	any
5.	blue	buy	city
6.	draw	four	great
7.	how	live	another
8.	boy	could	every
9.	far	from	hurt
10.	over	out	these

____/30

Name ________________________ Date ________________

1.	answer	brown	country
2.	start	then	there
3.	wash	went	who
4.	your	above	began
5.	different	enough	few
6.	grow	they	were
7.	which	why	follow
8.	girl	head	idea
9.	kind	leave	might
10.	next	often	paper

____/30

Name ______________________________ Date ____________________

1.	point	river	second
2.	song	think	three
3.	until	watch	white
4.	young	add	between
5.	close	example	food
6.	group	hear	home
7.	left	mountain	music
8.	night	old	picture
9.	sentence	spell	thought
10.	together	while	world

____/30

Quick Check
#183

Name ______________________ Date ______________

1.	air	along	begin
2.	children	important	letter
3.	open	own	sound
4.	talk	almost	animal
5.	around	body	color
6.	eye	form	high
7.	light	story	across
8.	become	complete	during
9.	happened	hundred	problem
10.	toward	study	wind

____/30

Quick Check
#184

Name ______________________ Date ______________

1.	against	certain	door
2.	early	field	heard
3.	knew	listen	morning
4.	several	area	ever
5.	hours	measure	notice
6.	order	piece	short
7.	today	true	covered
8.	cried	figure	horse
9.	money	products	question
10.	since	usually	voice

____/30

Quick Check
#185

Name ______________________ Date ______________

1.	able	behind	carefully
2.	common	easy	fact
3.	remember	sure	vowel
4.	whole	ago	government
5.	half	machine	pair
6.	quickly	scientist	thousand
7.	understood	wait	among
8.	building	circle	decided
9.	finally	heavy	include
10.	nothing	special	wheel

____/30

Name ______________________________ Date ____________________

1.	brought	contain	front
2.	gave	inches	material
3.	noun	ocean	strong
4.	verb	built	correct
5.	inside	island	language
6.	oh	person	street
7.	system	warm	dark
8.	clear	explain	force
9.	minutes	object	plane
10.	power	produce	surface

____/30